Western Barbary: Its Wild Tribes And Savage Animals

Sir John Hay Drummond-Hay

MOROCCO AND THE MOORS.

WESTERN BARBARY:

ITS

WILD TRIBES AND SAVAGE ANIMALS.

BY JOHN H. DRUMMOND HAY,

H. B. M. MINISTER IN MOROCCO.

NEW EDITION.

LONDON:

JOHN MURRAY, ALBEMARLE STREET.

1891.

LONDON :
PRINTED BY WILLIAM CLOWES AND SONS, LIMITED,
STAMFORD STREET AND CHARING CROSS.

INTRODUCTION.

THE journey which forms the groundwork of this small volume was undertaken for the purpose of procuring for Her Majesty, Queen Victoria, a barb of the purest blood from some of the breeders of horses in the region around Laraiche.

The Author, as the reader will perceive, was not so fortunate as to succeed in this object; but during the course of his expedition, short as it was, he saw such striking pictures of Arab life, and heard so many anecdotes illustrative of the peculiarities of character, customs, and manners in the various tribes, that he was tempted to commit them to writing.

Western Barbary possesses many points of interest, and has of late years been little explored by Europeans; but the Author has no intention, on the present occasion at least, to enter into any geographical or statistical details: his object in the following pages being merely to portray the character and manners of the wild tribes which inhabit this fertile but neglected country; and he has attempted to do this, not only by giving his own description of men and things, but by recording the wild and fanciful stories which were related to him by the Arab companions of his journey.

A residence of many years at Tangier, at which place his father is her Majesty's Consul-general, enabled the Author to become perfectly familiar with the Mogrebbin dialect of the Arabic; and he passed many weeks with the rude sportsmen of the country in their hunting expeditions into the interior. During these excursions he lived as they did, and became for the time one of their wild troop; and he thus acquired a considerable insight into their peculiarities of character.

The reader may perhaps be startled at the style, and the apparent admixture of fiction, in some of the stories given in this volume: but the Author can vouch for his having recorded with perfect accuracy and truth what was narrated to him. It would have been utterly impossible for him to have given a just idea of the feelings and tone of mind of the Moors, unless he had retained their romantic and exaggerated expressions; more especially as with them the most common occurrences of life are coloured with the highest tints of fancy, and every event is attributed to the direct interference either of the Supreme Being or of some tributary spirit.

In the habit also, which is universal amongst them, of relating long conversations with lions, boars, and hyænas, a Moorish sportsman scarcely considers that he is dealing in fiction; for, with him, every variety of sound which a wild animal utters is translatable into good Arabic.

CONTENTS.

CHAPTER I.

CHAPTER VIII.

CHAPTER IX.

CHAPTER X.

CHAPTER XI.

CHAPTER XII.

CHAPTER XIII.

CHAPTER XIV. (APPENDIX.)

WESTERN BARBARY.

CHAPTER I.

Departure from Tangier — The Gate-keeper — Moorish Guard — Outer Market-place — Burial-ground — The Ambassador's Road — Village of Swany—Description of Party—Village of Baharein—Hadj Amar—The Owner of the Rat-tailed—His Story of Alee the Six-fingered—Alee's Parentage—Marriage Feast—Feats of Alee—Lab el Barode—Firing at a mark—A dead Shot—Seedy Tayeb's Prophecy and Advice—Cruelty of Kaid Absalam—Alee victorious—The Vineyards of Bendeeban are robbed —The Thief discovered—A Father's Threat—Alee disappears—Feast in Marocco—Birth of a Prince—Mountebanks—The Swordsman Shasha's Challenge—Our Hero again—Appears before the Sultan.

"PRAYER is better than sleep! God is great!"—These words, chanted by the hoarse voice of the Mueddin * from a neighbouring mosque, had just roused me from my dreams, when our old guard, Kaid E'Soosy, entered my room, and, as he lighted my lamp, exclaimed, " Have you not a long day's journey before you, and are you still in bed?"

I was soon dressed, and quickly completed my preparations for a start.

It was on the morning of the 15th of August, 1839, as the first rays of light shot over Gibel Moossa,† the African Pillar of Hercules, that our little party set forth from Tangier, " the city protected of the Lord," on a visit to the wise Fakee,‡ the mighty Basha Abd E'Slam E'Slowy, then residing at Laraiche.

As we passed through the *Sok Srare* (the little market-place), groups of tall Reefians,§ enveloped in their white haiks or hooded gelab, the long mountain-dagger slung by their side, their heads

---

* The priest who announces the hour of prayer from the minaret.
† Ape's Hill.   ‡ A learned man.
§ The inhabitants of the line of mountains between Ceuta and Oran.

bare and closely shaved, with the exception of a long lock hanging wildly on their shoulders, were resting on their *Agarzeen,* or
Moorish hoes, waiting for hire; whilst every now and then there
passed by with measured steps a Taleb (Moorish scribe), returning from his matins in the great mosque, the living image of
those "who enlarged the borders of their garments, and loved
greetings in the market-place."*

We passed the Upper Fountain, where black slaves were
screaming and squabbling as to who should first fill their
antique-looking jars; whilst the Jew, the slave of slaves, waited
humbly until his acknowledged superiors of Islam were satisfied.

As we reached the gates of the town, old Hamed Ben Khajjo,
the porter, made his appearance. In one hand he carried a pon-
derous bunch of ancient-looking keys; in the other a rosary,
which he continued to finger, muttering away, as he counted his
beads, some of the ninety-nine epithets of the Deity—"O Giver
of Good to all! O Creator!" And then another bead; and
then a curse on the great-great-grandfathers of the crowd, who
pressed upon him. The heavy half-rotten gates, covered in part
with camel-skin, much of which had been devoutly cut off for
charms or medicinal purposes, swung back groaning on their
hinges, and we passed out.

Between the first and second barrier there is an open space
occupied by the forges and shops of smiths, and on the left a
nook, where formerly the bluff soldiers of our Charles II.† kept
their main-guard, but where now snored the lazy Moorish sen-
tinel, and some four or five long guns hung suspended in their
dusty covers.

The second gates were now thrown open, a long bolt being
their only fastening, the lock having been for years out of repair.
Nevertheless the old porter thought it expedient to go through
some form with a rusty key in the presence of "the Nazarene,
the rebeller against God and enemy of the Faithful."

"A safe journey to you, O son of the English!" said Hamed:
"Where are you going?"

"*Eeftah Allah*" (God will show), I answered, as my horse

* Matthew xxiii. 5-7.
† Tangier was possessed by the English in 1662, and was given up in
1684. It was received as part of the dowry of the Infant of Portugal.

bounded through the gate, and we found ourselves in the outer market and fairly started on our journey.

A long train of camels, driven by a half-naked Arab, were moving up the market-hill; a simple *Keiton*, or travelling-tent, was pitched near Seedy Mekhfee's sanctuary, the patron saint of the market-place, where a grey-bearded Arab was prostrating himself at his morning prayers: half a dozen donkeys completed the scene.

Ascending the hill, we passed through the Mohamedan burial-ground. Simple mounds of earth were crowded on either side of our path, all so placed as to point to the Prophet's tomb at Mecca. Most of them had a small board at the head; but those of the wealthier class were surrounded by a low and whitened wall; whilst here and there was seen an ancient tombstone, carved in arabesque, a monument of their formidable ancestors. Low palmetto bushes, some wild vines, creeping over a few solitary and blighted fig-trees, form the scanty ornaments of the Tangier cemetery.

Carefully I avoided treading on the graves, for it is said the souls of the Faithful are troubled when an infidel trespasses on their place of rest. Here it is that on Friday, the Mohamedan sabbath, the dark-eyed Houris of Tangier are seen, enveloped in their white haiks, and flitting like shrouded ghosts about the tombs. Wailing and lamentation are heard on every side; and the young widow may be often seen scattering myrtle on the grave of her husband, while, bending over it, she calls to him who can no longer hear:—"Oh! why have you deserted me? Have I been wanting in my duties to you, that I deserved so hard a fate? Woe, woe is me; I am left alone and wretched! why was not I freed with thee from the troubles of this life?" In other spots you see mothers bewailing the loss of their children, beating their breasts and sobbing aloud. Then come upon your ear the solemn chant and hurried footsteps of some funeral procession. The simple rites of the dead are performed in haste. Azrael, the angel of death, is supposed to be hovering over the fresh-dug grave, and any delay would be an infringement of the law of the Prophet.

We now reached the broad road of the Ambassadors, so called from being that by which all persons returning from missions to the Sultan enter the town; being the widest, and therefore most fit to receive the troops that may be sent to discharge their coarse powder in the faces of those on whom they are ordered to confer this great honour. On either side the road are vineyards and gardens, the hedges of which are variously formed of prickly pear, of the elegant cane, and formidable aloe, whose stately stems, covered with clusters of yellow flowers, compensate in some degree, at this season, for the want of trees in the scenery of this country. As we passed the *Kooba*, or alcoved tomb of Seedy Mohamed Al Hadj, the patron saint of Tangier, my soldier Mallem Ahmed muttered a fervent prayer, promising the sacrifice of a kid, should we have a safe return.

We soon traversed the few enclosures that surround the town, and then an extensive tract of open country lay before us. Hill after hill of half-cultivated land rose in succession, overtopped in the east by the heights of Anjĕra; and to the south and west the lofty mountain of Gibel Habeeb, the ranges of Beni Hoosma and Beni Hassen, which are the north-western feet of mighty Atlas, reared their lofty heads, which, now gilded by the rising sun, formed a grand framework for the landscape.

The morning was delightful; and a pleasant breeze, blowing from the south-west, the direction in which we were travelling, made the air cool, notwithstanding the burning rays of an African sun.

The village of Swany, the first we passed, and distant about a mile and a half from Tangier, is composed of sixty or seventy huts of sun-dried bricks, thatched with straw or reeds, on many of which stands within her nest the sainted stork, in full confidence, although raised but a few feet above a rabble rout of noisy children. Numerous cattle were grazing around on the sunburnt grass, whilst their herdsman, a wretched being in a tattered garb, soothed their sorry meal by a plaintive tune on his rude pipe, made of the country cane.

Here we were joined by my friend Hadj Abdallah, sheikh of the village, who had engaged to accompany me in my expedition, being a good judge of horses, and a man upon whom I could depend—a rarity in Marocco.

But before proceeding with my narrative, it is right that I should describe our little party. First comes our soldier, Mallem

Ahmed, the sole escort, who was mounted on a stout chesnut horse, and dressed in the flowing haik, over which was his soolham of blue cloth ; the tall red Moorish cap, with many folds of muslin gracefully twisted round it, formed his turban; and a pair of dandily worked yellow boots, with a terrific-looking pair of spurs, completed his dress. He had a good expression of countenance; his complexion was that of the south of Spain, with a scanty black beard, of which he took great care.

My friend the Hadj was mounted on a bat horse that carried our little tent. The Hadj is about six feet two inches, a fine specimen of the thorough-bred Reefian ; he wore a black gelab,* with a large turban, and the long Reefian knife was stuck in his girdle. A fierceness of features, blended with much kindliness of expression, formed the character of a countenance that is not uncommon among these highlanders. He was full of anecdote, and inconceivably fond of talking.

Then comes Sharky, my Jack-of-all-trades, my servant, my cook, my groom, my huntsman, my second soldier, but my prime minister in all my proceedings with the Moors. He was mounted on a monster of a mule, who carried the rest of our baggage, consisting of the carpet-bags, a mat and carpet, a few bottles of wine, and other small matters necessary for a Christian, and not to be got for love or money in an Arab *dooar*, or encampment. A Spanish friend yclept Don José M. Escazena,† and *Jan*, as the Moors call me, brought up the rear.

Our road, or rather track, *treck*, as the Arabs say, was good at this season of the year, though occasionally we gave our nags their heads to pick the way over deep cracked soil, which yawned for moisture. Undulating hills of a rich dark soil, patched here and there with yellow stubble, or the green crops of maize and dra, surrounded us on every side; and the deep gullies that lay across our route, down which run torrents of water in the rainy season, were now dry beds of rock and gravel.

* A coarse woollen dress worn by the lower orders, and similar in form to the cowl of monks. The early Christians probably adopted this fashion from the people of the East, among whom also it is found.

† Don José M. Escazena, who, by the by, approved himself the best possible of travelling companions, is an accomplished artist. In the course of our route he filled his portfolio with a series of very interesting sketches, the whole of which he kindly presented to me. Don José is now resident at Gibraltar.

We soon ascended the hill of *Băhărein,* or the Two Seas, so called from the Mediterranean and Atlantic being both seen from its summit. Some hundred yards to our right was a large village bearing the same name. Several smaller villages are situated in its neighbourhood, the huts of which, like all which I saw in this district, have each a small garden or orchard, enclosed with a hedge of prickly pears, giving them a picturesque appearance and almost an air of comfort.

" May God assist you, Hadj Amar ! " I said, addressing myself to a fine-looking Saracen, who advanced towards our party with a large bowl of milk, the emblem of peace : " and how fares your dog Dooah? When again shall we have a run with him after the boar in the plains of Sheref al Akaab ?"

At the sound of his name, a large hound, somewhat resembling our British greyhound, though stronger built, bounded forward, leaping up to my horse.

" He will never forget you," said his master, " O son of the English, after that last run in the Shreewa. What a thunderbolt of a boar that was ! Nothing but the book of fate saved my dog. But drink this milk—it will do you good."

" *Bismillah* " (in the name of God), I said, and put the bowl to my lips, and then handed it to our party.

" God will repay you ! " cried they, as we rode on.

" A path of peace to you," replied Hadj Amar ; " and let us have some days of hunting when you return."

We had passed the village about two miles, the Mallem was singing some ancient Mauro-Spanish ballad of love and wine, and I was conversing with my Christian friend on the mixture of good and evil in the character of the Moors—when " *Salamoo aleekoom*" (peace be with you) was uttered in the rear by some strange voice. We turned round to look at the speaker. He was a venerable-looking Arab, well mounted on an iron-grey rat-tailed barb ; on the bow of his high-peaked saddle rested the long Moorish gun ; and in his right hand he carried a small stick, upon which were inscribed some Arabic characters. This I recognised as one of the holy batons given by sainted persons to those who are about to undertake a journey, as a protection on the road from robbers and from mishaps of all sorts. A simple haik was his only covering ; his legs and sinewy arms were bare, and his slippered feet were armed with the Moorish spurs, which are merely silvered spikes of iron about a foot long, with a circle of metal at the hilt to prevent more than the point penetrating: but even with this precaution I have heard of a bad rider giving a death-wound to his steed.

"Whither, my friend, are you journeying?" said I to him: "I trust it be our way, since you have received that highly gifted blessing from some holy man, whose days, as well as yours, may God prolong!—and ours too, if you please!"

"Ah! Nazarene," said the owner of the rat-tailed, "you speak the Arabic! There is no knowing what you Christians have not learnt—God's will be done!—but this is your paradise: ours is to come. I am on my road to the tribe of Oolad Ensair (the Sons of the Eagle), whose tents are pitched some two days' journey south of Laraiche. As to this baton," he added, kissing it reverently as he spoke, "it was given me many years past by the father of the shereef Mulai Alee Bengeloon, the saint of Alcassar—on whom be peace! Nay, in truth, I have ever journeyed free from harm, even when Alee Boofrahee, the six-fingered—God preserve us from such another!—infested these regions. Christian, you have heard of Alee Boofrahee? Truly he was the wonder and terror of the world. But, poor fellow, what a dreadful death he suffered! May God have mercy on his soul!"

"Alee Boofrahee," said I, "the famous robber? They tell me miraculous stories of him."

"Allah!" exclaimed the stranger: "You would not believe me—May a ball pass through your heart, and a curse on your great-grandfather, for stumbling, you brute!" he exclaimed, addressing the rat-tailed—"You would not believe me, Christian, should I relate all his adventures."

"In truth," said I, "if you will slacken the pace of your horse, which seems to be a rare stepper, I should wish for nothing better than such a tale told by such a companion as you.

The Arab took me at my word, and accepting my compliment with a gracious bow, thus abruptly commenced his tale of the robber :—

"In the name of the most merciful God!—Know then, Nazarene, that some twenty years ago, when Moolai Soleeman was shaded by the imperial umbrella, there resided in the village of Bendeeban, which is situated on the way to Fas, about four miles south of Tangier, the father of our hero, Mohamed Boofrahee by name. Alee was his only son, his mother having gone to her Creator on the day of his birth, and Mohamed had vowed never to wed again.

" Mohamed Boofrahee, like the rest of his neighbours, was a poor farmer possessing two or three patches of land and a small vineyard. He was also a sportsman and a good shot. His young son Alee was never so happy as when accompanying his father on a shooting excursion, and he was always the first to see the game; for his father being now passed threescore, his sight had grown dim. An idle fellow was Alee in other respects; for though Mohamed sent him every morning to the village school to be instructed by Taleb Moostafa in the Koran, he was never able to repeat ten verses together of that holy book: but in running, playing at foot-ball, wrestling, or firing at a mark, no young man in the village could compete with the six-fingered.

" I remember," continued the rider of the rat-tailed, " on the marriage of Sheikh Mohamed Biteewy, of the village of Boamar, I was invited with my brethren, who were encamped in the plains of Sheref al Akaab, to attend the marriage-feast; and a merry-making, I can assure you, we had. God's bounty was seen in those days. There were dishes of Kesksoo* set before us which seven men could hardly lift; and the slave of the sheikh, the long-armed Embàrek, bared himself to the shoulder and dived into the deep dishes for the fat mutton, the goodly capons, and the other dainty bits. Water-melons, grapes, and other fruits were piled before us to sharpen appetite: drums and pipes sounded from daybreak to sunset, whilst the graceful Absalam enchanted the eyes of all, whilst they gazed on his gazelle-formed limbs, as he kept time in the dance to the guitar of Ben Daw-wed.

" *Lab el Barode* (powder-play) commenced. Our tribe mustered about two hundred horse; we charged in line: some stood on their heads at full speed; others changed horses with their

---

* The national dish of the Moors. It is made of the fine part of wheaten flour, and is dressed in a similar manner to Turkish pilaph—only steamed, instead of boiled.

companions at full gallop: then reining in, as we dashed within a gun's length of the sheikh, we fired our muskets, wheeled round, and gave place to others who charged close in our rear."

Here my new acquaintance, excited by the recital of the exploits of his tribe, suddenly broke off his story, and dashing his spurs into the flank of his barb, burst away at full speed, shouting " Allah! Allah! " His turban fell off—not accidentally, I am inclined to think—and the haik, loosed from his shoulders in the breeze, was poised in the air for a moment, and fell to the ground. He then fired, threw the rat-tailed on his haunches, and, wheeling round, came back at full gallop. As he approached us, he recovered his haik with the muzzle of his gun, and then throwing himself on one side, stretched his long arm, and, while yet in full course, whisked up his turban from the ground. In another moment he was by my side, replaced his head-gear with the greatest gravity, and continued his narrative as coolly as if he had merely paused to take a pinch of snuff.

"The powder-play," said he, "being finished, we fired at a mark. Seedy Tayeb Boocassem of Wazan, whom God had blessed with an unerring eye—the prince of marksmen—chanced to be present. To him we referred to judge who amongst us was the best shot. A pile of stones, with a small pebble or a flower at the top, was our target. Many good shots had been made, but the beardless Alee put us all to shame; seldom did he miss the flower, and Boocassem declared him to be the victor. When the firing ceased, Boocassem offered up a prayer to the Lord of all creatures for the welfare of the whole party.

" ' Seedy Boocassem,' said the sheikh, ' there is one shot yet to be fired, and that too by the finest marksman amongst us : so get ready your gun. And here,' continued the sheikh, holding out an egg, ' who is there that will put this egg between his ankles, and stand by yonder aloe for Seedy Tayeb Boocassem to break it ? '

" There was a dead silence—no one moved from his place but young Alee. The boy ran forward, kissed the hand of Sheikh Mohamed Biteewy, and soon placed himself at the aloe with the egg between his ankles.

" ' In the name of God,' said Boocassem, as he poured in the powder, and rammed down the wadding of palmetto rind;

and ' God be propitious,' said he, as the ball rolled down.   The
cock of the gun was pulled back, the priming was poured into
the pan, and Boocassem, squatting on the ground, levelled his
gun.

    " ' Am I properly placed ? ' said Alee.

    " ' Bring up the left leg more ;' said Boocassem : ' that will do.'

    " The long gun seemed as steady as if it had rested on a rock :
every man held his breath.   Bang went the gun, and Alee's
ankles were besmeared with the yolk of the egg.

    " ' Thank God ! ' said Boocassem ; and we shouted one and all.

    " Young Alee came forward, and Seedy Tayeb Boocassem
laid his hands on him and blessed him, prophesying that at some
future time he also would be able to perform the feat of break-
ing the egg.   ' But beware, boy,' said he, ' attempting it until
you arrive at such perfection as never to miss your mark ; for I
remember, some years ago, when I was at the holy city of Wazàn
during the feast of the lamb, Bengeloon and other marksmen of
fame from distant parts had assembled to shoot at the target.
Bengeloon and I were the only two who had fired at the egg.
Then Kaid Absalam, he who had been governor of Alcassar,
whose heart was black with envy, swore by the beard of our
Prophet that he could do what others had done before him : so
he called one of his slaves, and told him to take his place with
the egg, about thirty paces from where he was sitting :—it was
the same distance at which we had fired.

    " The gun was levelled, and Bengeloon—may 'God profit us
through him !—looking over the kaid's shoulder, exclaimed,
' Allah ! unless you keep your gun steadier, O kaid, you will hit
his left leg.'   Bang went the gun, and the slave fell with a
groan, for the ball had passed through his left ankle.

    " ' There go a hundred dollars,' said Kaid Absalam ; ' but the
next shot shall hit the egg.   Abd-el-Habeeb,' said he, calling on
another of his slaves, ' take another egg, and stand where Em-
barek stood.   Coward ! what do you tremble for ?   Stand steady,
or I will put a ball through your heart.'

    " Again the gun was levelled.

    " ' All wrong,' said Bengeloon, who remained at his shoulder.
Bang it went, and the ball passed through the fleshy part of the
leg, but the slave kept his position.

" 'That is a fine fellow,' said Bengeloon to the kaid, who was again loading his gun: ' Be merciful, as you expect mercy in the world to come.'

" 'True,' said the kaid, ' but I must have another shot, for all that.' He fired for the third time, and broke the egg!"

" Well, Christian, as soon as Seedy Tayeb Boocassem finished his story, wrestling and playing at sword-stick commenced:— Alee threw and overcame every antagonist; and the marriage feast ended merrily.

" Days and months rolled on, and Alee was idle, and would not work with his father. The grape season came, and it was found that the vineyards of Bendeeban had been plundered; but the robber could not be discovered: although a sharp look-out was kept constantly from the tall aloe-stalk watch-stands both night and day, the thief eluded all their vigilance.

" One morning Mohamed Boofrahee, Alee's father, having gone into his own vineyard, observed a quantity of the fruit to be missing. Mohamed, who, as I have already told you, was a sportsman, and accustomed to track his game, searched for the footsteps of the plunderer; but the ground was hard and dry— no traces could be found, and he was giving up all search as use-less, when on one spot a well known footmark caught his eye. ' Holy Prophet!' exclaimed Mohamed, as he counted the marks of the toes, one, two, three, four, five, six; ' have I not forbidden Alee to enter the vineyard? Ah! it is he who has robbed the vineyard of my neighbours as well as his father's. This comes of idleness.'

" Mohamed returned home sorrowful; Alee was an only son, and he was proud of him.

" ' Alee,' said his father, as they sat alone that night, ' you have been in the vineyard.' Alee did not answer. ' Alee,' re-peated his father, ' you had my orders never to enter that place. I have now discovered who is the plunderer of Bendeeban's vines. But justice shall be done, and to-morrow I shall give you over to the sheikh to receive due punishment. Your idle disposition has long been a cause of distress to me—a good bas-tinado may help to cure you.'

" Mohamed parted with Alee that night in anger. The morn-ing dawned; Mohamed was doatingly fond of his son; he had changed his mind, and thought it better to hush up the matter, but he resolved to give him some good advice as to his future conduct. So he called out loudly for him, but Alee was not to be found. That day passed and the next; and weeks, and months, and years elapsed, yet still his son was missing.

" Some six years after, there was a great feast in the city of Marocco; the sultan's favourite wife, Làlà Fàtima, had been brought to bed of a son, and an imperial order was given that there should be three days of rejoicing; and a countless throng of Arabs and Berbers flocked into the city. It was on the second morning of this feast, and a great crowd had collected to gaze at some mountebanks, who abound on such occasions. Some people were standing, some few behind the rest were on horseback, but the far greater part were squatted on their hams. It was in the vast market-place of Marocco, not far from the stately tower of the great mosque,* the Kootsabeea which stands towering above the countless minarets, and whence the unity of God and Mohamed's mission are daily proclaimed.

" There were snake-charmers from the desert, jugglers from Soos, and story-tellers in abundance; but what most attracted attention was a tall athletic black from the Bokhàry body-guard of the sultan, who had challenged six men to cudgel-play, all the six at once; and was now brandishing a long staff against that number of antagonists, all armed with the like weapon and all active players. But the black, by his superior vigour and won- derful dexterity, evaded all their onsets, dealing every now and then, as a momentary occasion offered, a blow that came like a flash of lightning on each opponent.

" Each man, when he received a hit from the swarthy athlete, retired from the ring—the rule being such. The black had al- ready disposed of three, and by keeping constantly on the move, and giving every now and then the spring of an antelope, he re- mained himself untouched. The three unhit fencers were men of skill and power, and now with united assaults they pressed hard upon him, but he found victory in pretended flight; for thus separated, the three became, each in his turn, easy victims to his unequalled prowess.

* Like in construction to that of the Girelda of the Cathedral at Seville, and built by the same famous Geber.

" Flushed with success, the Bokhàry conqueror bared his brawny arm, and now shouted a challenge, that was heard from Bab-el-khamees to Bab-el-khadar,* against all comers; daring any man to receive and give one blow with the fist.

" This same challenge had been repeatedly made on former feasts, and few had ever accepted it with impunity; for a broken rib or some other serious injury always attended a blow from the champion, who was a perfect tower of strength, and the chief of the Blow-givers.†

" A broad-shouldered, athletic-looking fellow, in the garb of a mountaineer, stepped forward and accepted the challenge, on condition that, 'if God gave him the victory,' security should be assured him from the resentment of the Bokhàry's comrades.

" That the challenge of the chief Blow-giver had been accepted, reached the ears of the sultan, who sent for the mountaineer, and asked him whether it were true that he dared to engage in combat the mighty Shasha, who dealt in blows of death.

" ' May God prolong the life of our master !' said the mountaineer, throwing himself at the feet of the descendant of the Prophet : ' Yes, my lord, I have accepted the challenge of the kaid ‡ of the Blow-givers, on condition that I be secured from the vengeance of the Bokhàry, should God grant me success.'

" ' You are a sturdy looking fellow,' said the sultan : ' where do you come from, and what is your name ?'

" ' Alee Boofrahee,' replied the man, for he it was; and throwing himself prostrate, he told his tale, but said nothing about Bendeeban's vineyard.

" He had employed himself, it appeared, as courier and muleteer since his flight from his father's house, and had led a roving life, having travelled throughout the whole empire.

" ' Let him be lodged in the palace,' said the sultan to his at-

* Two opposite gates of the city of Marocco.
† Among the household soldiery of the Moorish sultan, there are certain men charged with particular services, which they alone can perform. Their titles are—mwal-ei-asà, the blow-giver; mwal-ayfel, the scourgers; mwal-sekkeen, the swordsmen; mwal-mkahel, the shooters; mwal-emzergeen, the spearmen. These officers are alone authorized to strike, scourge, cut, shoot, or spear, the sultan's faithful and loving subjects, as the fancy of their imperial master may dictate when he appears amongst them.
‡ The chief.

tendants: 'to-morrow, if it please the most high God, the blows shall be given in our Shereefian* presence.'

"The guards fell prostrate, their heads touching the ground, crying out as they did so, 'May God prolong the life of our master!' Then they led off Alee, who that night had his heart's content of kesksoo."

* Of Prophetic origin.

CHAPTER II.

Journey continued—Thrashing Corn—Relic of Idolatry—Ain Dàlla—Cross the Mhaha—Advice of the owner of the filly—Arab's love for his horse—Dar-al-Clow—Bagging a Jackal—Boar-hunt—Death of a Hound—Funeral Mound.

I INTERRUPTED our new acquaintance in his story, to point out to my Spanish friend some Moors thrashing corn. Mares with their colts tied abreast by the head or neck are used for this work. One man stands in the middle holding the reins, whilst another shouts and applies the whip or goad when necessary. Mules and donkeys are employed in bringing the sheaves.

The country folk are dressed in light woollen shirts, their arms and legs bare; a red cap or small turban covers the head; their shoes are religiously left at the margin of the thrashing-floor, it being regarded as holy ground by all the children of the East. I remarked that they carefully avoid making any calculation of the produce of their harvest, and are offended if you question them as to their expectations, checking you by the grave reply—" As God may please."

There is a curious custom which seems to be a relic of their pagan masters, who made this and the adjoining regions of North Africa the main granary of their Latin empire. When the young corn has sprung up, which it does about the middle of February, the women of the villages make up the figure of a female, the size of a very large doll, which they dress in the gaudiest fashion they can contrive, covering it with ornaments to which all in the village contribute something; and they give it a tall peaked head-dress. This image they carry in procession round their fields, screaming and singing a peculiar ditty. The doll is borne by the foremost woman, who must yield it to any one who is quick enough to take the lead of her; which is the cause of much racing and squabbling. The men also have a similar custom, which they perform on horseback. They call the image *Mata*.

These ceremonies are said by the people to bring good luck. Their efficacy ought to be great, for you frequently see crowds of men engaged in their performance, running and galloping recklessly over the young crops of wheat and barley.

Such customs are directly opposed to the faith of Islam, and I never met with a Moor who could in any way enlighten me as to their origin.

The Berber tribes, the most ancient race now remaining in these regions, to which they gave the name, are the only ones which retain this antique usage, and it is viewed by the Arabs and dwellers in the town as a remnant of idolatry.

We now passed by *Ain Dàlla*, the Fountain of the Vine, so called from this spot having been famous in days of yore for its grapes, but, like everything else in this country, it has gone to ruin, and not a vestige remains of ancient industry, except a few wild vines climbing over stunted fig-trees.

An Arab *dooar*, or encampment, is perched on the summit of the hill, composed of tents made of the palmetto fibre, and a few huts erected by those who, finding a rich pasturage and favourable soil, have here fixed their permanent abode.

After descending the hill we passed over a rich plain, and crossed the shallow bed of the river *Mhàhà*, the banks of which, all red with the flowers of the oleander, appeared at a distance like a stream of fire.

Having passed the river, we found ourselves in a sandy region, whence the country around takes the name of *Kàà Ermel*, or the plain of sand: it is, however, well irrigated by the winter rains, and thick stubbles of wheat and barley recently cut showed its fertility.

The Hadj called my attention to a fine filly feeding with her dam among the stubble. We halted to examine her; she was a three-year old, and a vastly pretty creature, with a head, the best point of barbs, so small that she might truly have drunk from a quart-pot. But her fore and hind legs had been sadly disfigured by firing: this is done by the Arabs at an early age; and, instead of being considered a defect, as with us, is held rather to increase the value of the animal.

A young Arab, half naked, rising from the stubble like an apparition, showed that the mare was not unguarded. Thinking I might be induced to buy her, he began to tell her lineage, and gravely informed me that the only disadvantage that would arise to her rider was, that he would be deafened if ever he put her at full speed. "But," said he, gravely, "you can remedy that by always putting cotton in your ears."

It is not always that the Arab is ready to part with his horse, if a good beast, whatever price may be offered; though money amongst the degraded people of Marocco will work miracles. A circumstance which proved this occurred to me about four years ago, when accompanying poor John Davidson* some few days' journey into the interior.

As we were proceeding between Mehedeea and Rabàt we were joined by a troop of mounted Arabs, one of whom was riding a mottled grey, the handsomest barb I ever saw.

Riding up to the man, I entered into conversation with him, and, having put him in good humour by praising his steed. I told him I would make him rich if he would sell me the mottled grey.

"What is your price?" said the Arab.

I offered a hundred and fifty *mitsakel*, about twenty pounds sterling, a large sum in the interior.

"It is a good price," said the Arab; "but look," said he, and he brought his horse on the other side of me,—"look at this side of him,—you must offer more."

"Well, come," I said, "you are a poor man, and fond of your horse; we won't dispute about the matter; so, give me your hand.†—What say you? two hundred?"

"That is a large price, truly," said the Arab, his eyes glistening, and I thought the horse was mine. But my eagerness, I suppose, had been too apparent, so the Arab thought I might go still further; and shaking the bridle, off he went at full speed. The mottled grey curled its tail in the air, and vanished to a speck in no time:—I turned to speak to Davidson, and the

---

* In the Appendix at the end of this volume will be found some particulars regarding this adventurous traveller, who met his death in 1836, in attempting to penetrate from Wadnoon to Timbuctoo.

† The Moorish manner of striking a bargain.

c

next moment the Arab was at my side; and patting the neck of his grey, he said, "Look at him—see—not a hair is turned! What will you give me now?"

Davidson prompted me to offer even four hundred ducats rather than let the animal go. Again I began bargaining, and offered three hundred. On this the Arab gave his hand, and thanking me, said—"Christian, I now can boast of the price you have offered; but it is in vain that you seek to tempt me, for I would not sell my horse for all the gold you, or any other man, possess." Having said this, he joined his companions.

Calling the kaid, or chief of our escort, I asked him if he knew the rider of the grey,—adding, that I supposed he must be rich, as he had refused so large a sum. The kaid said, "All I know is, that he is a great fool; for he possesses nothing in the world but that horse, which he bought when a colt, selling his tent, flocks, and even his wife, to buy it."

I think that I have read a tale similar to this in Malcolm's 'Sketches of Persia;' but what I have related occurred to myself, and precisely as I have described it.

Dar-el-Clow, a rugged sierra lying east and west, was now to be climbed, and we rode by a rocky path through a jungle of dwarf oak, cistus, white, rose, and yellow flowered laurestinus, arbutus, and myrtle. In our track lay the dead body of a camel. The animal, not formed by nature to climb such steeps, seemed to have broken its back. This happens, I understand, not unfrequently during the winter time, when the *kafflas*, the caravans of the West, attempt to travel during the rainy season. The poor creatures then become a prey to the jackals, packs of whom are ever on the watch for such disasters.

I remember a muleteer telling me he once had caught a couple of young jackals inside the carcass of a camel upon which he had come suddenly. Being surprised to hear a slight noise from within, he peered into the dead body, and there found *Taleb Yoosef* and his lady. So, taking off his gelab, he bagged them both.—The jackal, from his cunning, is called by the natives Taleb Yoosef (the scribe Joseph).

Strange to say, the Mohamedans of this country, though disgusted at the sight of pork, will feast upon the jackal as a delicacy.

This beast is not altogether carnivorous, for he eats with avidity the dates of the palmetto, and the berries of the arbutus and myrtle; and in this respect also resembles the fox, who, as is well known, is very fond of grapes when he can get them.

We were slowly winding up the hill, and I had just requested our new ally to resume his story of the Six-fingered, when we heard the well-known tongue of a boar-hound. "Hark!" said the Hadj—"Hark to old Zeitsoon!" I gave spurs to my horse, and was soon at the top of the hill, just in time to see a huge boar dash across the path, some fifty yards in front. Pell-mell at his heels came a motley pack of curs in full cry; and at a distance I heard the usual shouts of the beaters—"Get out, you Jew!" "At him, Zeitsoon!" "Hide yourself, Jawan!" "No other but the one God!"—and then many a long gun glistened through the bushes. I stood still until they came up, and soon recognised many old friends and fellow-hunters. They were half stripped, their legs well protected by palmetto buskins, formed exactly like the greaves of ancient Greece, with a leather apron to defend the body from the thorny thicket. Some with long guns, others with bill-hooks, to be used either to cut their way through the jungle, or, if need be, to defend themselves from the boar's onset, were following the dogs in ardent pursuit. A shot was heard upon our right, in the valley below, and in the direction that the boar had taken. They paused. By the note of the dogs they knew that the beast was at bay; so on dashed the whole hunt, shouting to their dogs to keep clear of the boar, and expressing their feelings in the most *endearing terms*. Such as "My children—My dearest—Take care, he sees you—He is an infidel, a Nazarene—He will have his revenge—None but the one God!"

The soldier with the baggage animals now joined me, and desiring him to go on to a well about a quarter of a mile off, where there was shade, and the Hadj and Sharky, both old hunters, also giving their animals to his care, we all rushed on into the thicket, and soon reached the spot where the shot had been fired: there we found a hale, though hoary hunter, who could not have weathered less than eighty winters, reloading his gun. He it was who had struck the boar.

The beast was at bay in a thicket of brambles, surrounded by the dogs and hunters; he showed great fight, but we soon dispatched him. He was a huge monster, and proved the truth of the poet's description—

> " On his bow back he hath a battel set
>   Of bristly pikes, that ever threat his foes:
> His eyes like glow-worms shine when he doth fret,
>   His snout digs sepulchres where'er he goes.
> Being moved, he strikes whate'er be in his way;
>   And whom he strikes, his crooked tushes slay."

Three of the dogs were wounded—one of them fatally. The poor animal had just life enough to wag his tail and raise his head as his owner, a fine young mountaineer, came up, and took him in his lap.

"Alas! my poor dog," he said; "did I not warn you not to go near the infidel? But God's will be done." The tears started in his eyes as his dog expired.

The bill-hooks were set to work, and a grave was dug to bury the poor animal; each man put a stone upon it, as a tribute of his affectionate regret, and I, on my part, added one to the number.

The wounds of the other two dogs were now sewn up—the thorn or point of the aloe leaf and its fibres being substituted for a surgeon's needle and silk thread.

A fire was lit, and the boar put on to roast for their dogs, they having first offered me the lion's portion, whilst a little sly joking passed amongst them at my expense, such as—" Let *Jan* have a larger portion than the other dogs."

I did not accept their offer, for I had no one who would cook me the pork; but I invited my friends to accompany me to the well, as the sun was now at its height, and scorching hot, promising them a supper of bread and fruit.

They readily accepted my invitation, and we toiled up the hill together, and re-entered the beaten track. Here and there mounds of stones marked the graves of unfortunate travellers, who on those spots had reached their goal of life. Their funeral monuments are raised by the pious hands of passers-by, according to the custom which has been in use from earliest times :—

> " Vagæ ne parce malignus arenæ
> Ossibus et capiti inhumato
> Particulam dare."— HORACE, *Carm.* i. 28.

And this relic of ancient usage is still found to exist in many and far-distant countries.

Here I threw my stone again, and so did each of the hunters as they passed, muttering a prayer for the soul of the departed: but, for all that, among my troop perhaps might be the very man who had committed the deed of blood on some one of those whose obsequies we celebrated; for my supper-party were as wild a set as could well have been collected together. Yet I felt safe among them, since I had often broken the bread of friendship, and shared with them in their toils and pleasures of the chace: in fact, they looked on me as a brother-sportsman; and, I believe, would have laid down their lives, rather than a hair of my head should be injured.

CHAPTER III.

Lion-hunting—The Punishment of a good Shot—Story of the Battle between
a Lion and a Boar—Affray with a Boar—My Story—The Melon Boar.

MALLEM HAMED had spread our carpets under the thick foliage
of the *Kharrob*, or locust-tree; and there the water-melons and
grapes—which were placed before us—soon disappeared amongst
the numerous party.

The sport of the day was discussed: and the old hunter who
had wounded the boar told us that he had been in some danger;
for the beast rushed at him as he fired, and it would have gone
hard with the veteran, if he had not sprung behind a tree.

" In truth," said the man, " I am an old lion-hunter; but I
have found more danger in hunting the boar than in pursuit of
the sultan of the forest; since with the lion one is always more
or less prepared for his attack."

He went on to tell us that in the country of Reef, where he
often hunted the lion, each man goes armed with a gun, a
dagger, and three or four iron-tipped stakes. A hole about four
feet in depth is dug, just wide enough for each man to crouch
down in. The stakes are then driven into the ground with their
iron points slightly inclined outwards; each sportsman, as in
boar-hunting, takes his station in these places of safety, which
are dug in the tracks of the lion.

The beaters, making a great noise with drums, and snouting
and firing of guns, drive the game towards the hunters: should
they wound the lion, he generally springs at the man that fired,
who immediately stoops, and the lion, falling on one of the
stakes, is dispatched with their daggers.

" You have," said I, " many lions in the region of *Akkalaya*.
I suppose it is dangerous to be out after dark?"

" They rarely attack a man, if unprovoked," replied the old
Reefian: " I have met them when alone; they have stood and

looked at me.   But in such cases a man must go on his way
without appearing to notice the beast, and then he will almost
always quietly walk away also."

" The best caution I can give," continued our grey-bearded
guest, " in case you ever meet a lion, is, that you should keep
on your own path with all the coolness you can command, until
you observe that the *yellow-haired* * has passed out of view or
has ceased watching you; then turn sharp to another direction,
and pursue it rapidly, lest the lion, having noticed the line of
your march, should proceed to meet you at a distance on that
track, as they often do with all the cunning of a cat; and you
may then have some difficulty in evading his wantonness or
anger."

This advice somewhat reminded me of the story of the old
peer, who, being asked what he had done on meeting a lion
in the Strand, which had broken loose from Exeter Change,—
replied with great composure—" Do? I called a coach."
Nevertheless I treasured up the advice against a future emer-
gency.

To my question, whether it was not very dangerous to hunt
lions without the precaution of the pit and stakes, our guest replied, " Yes, Christian, it is: you carry your life in your open
hand."

" I remember," continued he, " a son of the sheikh of our
village returned home one evening trailing along the skin of a
huge lion, which he laid at the feet of his father, and showing
the hole where the ball had penetrated the skull, he told the
sheikh that he had, alone, met the animal face to face in the
wood, and killed him.

" ' My son,' said the sheikh, ' with which finger did you pull
the trigger?'

" The young man held his forefinger up.

" ' Seize and bind him,' said the sheikh, and drawing his
knife said, ' I cut off that finger, my beloved, that you may
remember for the future, never to attack a lion when you are
alone; for I would not lose you, my son, for a thousand, no,
nor for ten thousand lion-skins.'

" In vain we all cried out to the sheikh to spare the youth,

* An Arabic expression, signifying a Lion.

who stood calmly obedient : but though the big tears rolled down the father's rugged cheeks, the finger was cut off."

" Do they destroy many of your cattle ? " I asked.

" Now and then a sheep," said the old Reefian, " and some-times a heifer if found alone ; but though during the summer we turn our cattle into the woods, we seldom lose any. At night, to guard against the lion, the cattle, of their own instinct, form a circle, in the centre of which remain the heifers and cows, and outside of these the bullocks, the bulls placing themselves as sentries round the fold. If any bull hear or wind a lion, he makes a lowing noise and paws with his feet ; the other bulls know the signal, and, forming themselves in line, dash at full speed on the spot where they suppose the lion to be, who gene-rally makes off from such formidable assailants. It is not an unknown thing for bulls to gore a lion to death. Gazelle deer and wild swine are the principal prey for the lion ; but with a full-grown boar he has often a tremendous conflict, and some-times the lion gets the worst of it ; as I shall show you, O son of the English ! " added the Reefian, " in a short tale of what I myself had the rare luck to witness when a very young man."

This announcement caused a general silence throughout the party ; and the veteran, looking round with an air of very con-siderable dignity and importance, thus began :—

" Now this is a story of the Boar and *two* Lions.

" In the days of my youth, when a black moustache curled where now you see the hoary beard of my winter's age, I seldom passed a night within my father's hut ; but sallying out with my gun, laid wait for the wild animals which frequented a neigh-bouring forest.

" One moonlight night I had taken my position on a high rock, which overhung a fountain and a small marsh, a favourable spot with our hunters to watch for boars, who resorted thither to drink and root.

" The moon had traversed half the heavens, and I, tired with waiting, had fallen into a doze, when I was roused by a rustling in the wood, as on the approach of some large animal. I raised myself with caution, and examined the priming of my gun, ere the animal entered the marsh. He paused and seemed to be listening, when a half growl, half bark, announced him to be a boar, and a huge beast he was, and with stately step he entered the marsh.

" I could now see by the bright moon, as he neared my station, that his bristles were white with age, and his tusks gleamed like polished steel among the dark objects round him. I cocked my gun, and waited his approach to the fountain.

" Having whetted his ivory tusks, he began to root; but he appeared to be restless, as if he knew some enemy was at hand; for every now and then raising his snout, he snuffed the air.

" I marvelled at these movements, for as the breeze came from a quarter opposite to my position, I knew I could not be the object of the boar's suspicions.

" Now, however, I distinctly heard a slight noise near the edge of the marsh : the boar became evidently uneasy; and I heard him say with a clear voice, for you must know they were formerly men, ' *I hope there is no treachery*.'

" This he repeated once or twice, and again began to root.

" Keeping a sharp look-out on the spot whence I heard the strange noise, I fancied I could distinguish the grim and shaggy head of a lion crouching upon his fore paws, and, with eyes that glared like lighted charcoal through the bushes, he seemed peering at the movements of the boar. I looked again, and now I could see plainly a lion creeping, cat-like, on his belly, as he neared the boar, who was busy rooting, but with bristles erect, and now and then muttering something that I could not understand.

" The lion had crept within about twenty feet of the boar, but was hidden in part by some rushes. I waited breathless for the result; and, although myself out of danger, I trembled with anxiety at the terrible scene.

" The boar again raised his snout, and half turned his side towards the lion, and I fancied I could see his twinkling eye watching the enemy. Another moment, and the lion made a spring, and was received by the boar, who reared up on his hind legs. I thought I could hear the blow of his tusks as the combatants rolled on the ground. Leaning over the rock, I strained my eyes to see the result. To my surprise the boar was again on his legs, and going back a few paces, rushed at his fallen foe : a loud yell was given by the lion, which was answered by the distant howlings of the jackals. Again and again the ferocious boar charged, till he buried his very snout in the body of the lion, who was kicking in the agony of death. Blood indeed flowed from the sides of the boar, but his bristles still stood erect as he triumphed over the sultan of the forest, and now he seemed to be getting bigger and bigger. ' God is great ! ' said I, as I trembled with dread : ' He will soon reach me on the rock.' I threw myself flat on my face, and cried out, ' There is no other God but God, and Mohamed is his prophet ! ' I soon recovered my courage, and looked again. The boar had returned to his natural size, and was slaking his thirst in the fountain. I seized my gun, but, reflecting, said within myself, ' Why should I kill him ? He will not be of any use to me ; he has fought bravely, and left me the skin of a lion, and perhaps he may be a Jin :' * so I laid down the gun, contenting myself with thoughts of the morrow.

" The boar had left the fountain, and was again busied rooting in the marsh, when another slight noise, as of a rustling in the wood, attracted my notice, and I could perceive the smooth head of a lioness looking with surprise and horror at the body of her dead mate.

" ' What ! treachery again !' said the boar in a low tone.

" ' God is great !' said the lioness ; ' but he shall pay for this ! What ! a pig ! an infidel ! to kill a lion ! One spring, and I will do for him.' Having said these words, she advanced boldly. The boar stood prepared, grinding his teeth with rage. She paused, and again retreated to the wood, and I could hear her say, ' O God ! all merciful Creator ! What an immense boar ! what an infidel ! what a Christian of a pig !'

" ' May God burn your great-great-grandmother,' said the boar.

" On hearing the creature *curse her* parent, she again stopped, and, lashing her tail, roared with a voice that the whole wood re-echoed, and she said, ' There is no conqueror but God.'

" The boar stamped his hoofs, and gnashed his tusks again with rage ; his grisly bristles, red with the blood of her mate, stood on end ; then, lowering his snout, he rushed headlong

* An evil genius or spirit.

against the lioness, who, springing aside, avoided the dread blow,
A cloud came over the moon; I could not see distinctly, but I
heard every blow of the paw and every rip of the tusk. There
was a dead silence; again the cloud had passed, and the heavens were clear, and I saw the lioness with her fore paws on the
body of the boar.

" I seized my gun, and aimed at her head; that was her last
moment.

" The morning dawned. I descended from the rock. The
claw of the lioness still grasped in death the body of the boar.
Many severe wounds showed that the boar had again fought
bravely.

" The lions were the finest I ever saw, and I made good
profit by that night's work."

We were still applauding the old hunter's story, when a gaunt
Arab, thrusting forward his bare and sinewy leg, exclaimed,
" Look at these scars, and keep in mind, O ye faithful, and
thou, O son of the English, that it is not only dogs that are
wounded or killed in chace of the *boar*."

" Let us hear how you got them," said the young mountaineer,
the owner of the dog that had been killed.

" It is soon told," said the man of scars.

" Some eight years past, during harvest-time, I was watching
at night for a boar in a field of ripe barley near *Ras Ashacár*,*
and had fired at a large boar, who reeled and fell, but got up
again and made away.

" At dawn of day I went to the spot where the animal had
fallen, and finding marks of blood, I traced them to some brushwood in the centre of the field, which spot I ringed, and, perceiving the animal had not gone away, I was thinking what
might be best to do, my gun cocked in my hand, when I heard a
rush, and before I could get the gun to my shoulder, the boar
was upon me; the gun was dashed out of my hand, and I expected every rip I received that my doom had been written. God
knows how long this encounter lasted; the time seemed to be as
an age.

" Finding no manner of escape, I slipped my arms from the

* Cape Spartel.

gelab, and escaped out, leaving the animal to vent his rage on my garment. I crawled off, but fainted from loss of blood.

"I did not recover my senses till I was found by my family, who carried me home to *Mesnàna*,* half dead. I told my story there, and a party of hunters went out directly to revenge my wounds. They found the beast had again retreated to his lair, having cut my dress into shreds. He attacked them as he had done myself, but they were prepared, and soon killed him. I was not able to stand on my legs for many months after."

"The son of the English," said Sharky, pointing to me, "had just as narrow an escape four years ago, when he and the son of America attacked a boar at bay."

"Let us hear," said they all, "O Nazarene!"

I complied with their request, and, suiting my style to my audience, told my tale much after the following fashion:—

"It was in the month of October, O ye faithful children of the Prophet, and early in the morning, that I received a message from the son of America, who had passed the night in the hills watching for boar, begging me to join him at the marshes of Boobána as soon as possible, and to bring my hunter Sharky, with his two dogs, and an *extra* gun. The messenger told me that my friend had wounded a large boar; and that, while tracking him, the animal had rushed from the thicket; that his rifle had missed fire; and that, had it not been for a ruined wall on which he had taken refuge, he would have fared badly.

"I soon joined my friend, whom I found still perched on the topmost point of the wall waiting my arrival.

"The boar had moved off to some distance in the thicket. We soon got on the track of the beast, and found, by the print of his hoofs, that he was wounded on the right hind leg.

"'At him, *Merkis*,' said Sharky, as he slipped his dogs. 'Get out, you Jew! There is only one God!' Which the old hound *Zeitsoon* answered by *bow*; and the little cur *Merkis*, whose hide was striped like a zebra's from the rips of boars, yelped with joy as he got on the scent.

"'That's him,' shouted Sharky. 'None but the one God!'

"The dogs had now headed us some hundred yards, when we

* A village near Tangier

heard *Zeitsoon* give tongue, as when the boar is at bay; and it was quite certain that this was a large one, for both the dogs seemed to be keeping at a respectful distance.

" I had scrambled through the thicket within some few yards of the place where the dogs were giving tongue, and was calling to my companions to know where they were, in case I fired; but the only answer I received, O ye faithful, was given me by the boar, who was nearer than I had imagined. Luckily I had kept clear of his path; so he dashed by within a few paces of me, without my being able to get a shot, or he a rip. The dogs followed in full cry, and had reached an open space, when we heard a piteous howl. I made for the spot. Poor *Zeitsoon* had been almost severed in half. The boar, we supposed, had laid in wait for him in the open space.

" Sharky, when he saw the frightful state of his brave and faithful hound, sat down, without saying a word, and, taking his turban, began to bind up the wound, whilst he offered up a prayer for the life of the poor dog. The boar had now managed to make his way up the opposite bank; and little *Merkis*, heedless of his companion's fate, yelped on the track; when again a howl grated on our ears. Sharky started up on his feet, and, brandishing his bill-hook, shouted to the full extent of his lungs, 'Hide yourself, *Merkis*. Do not trust him. He is an infidel.'

" The dog showed he was not much hurt, by still giving tongue, though in such a manner as told us that the boar had again come to bay.

" Having called a council of war, my friend and I determined to go in to the boar by ourselves, as more than two persons would only create confusion.

" The enraged beast had come to bay in a jungle of gum-cistus, entangled with briers—a very unfavourable place for our attack. However, having thrown off our shooting-jackets, and examined the priming of our guns, we entered the wood, agreeing to keep some few paces from each other.

" At first we made against the wind, and kept clear of the boar-paths, which is the best method of avoiding an unexpected attack. Having advanced some way through the thicket, I was obliged to return to a boar-path, for I found it was impossible to make way through the brambles, having already left most of my covering among the thorns.

" I moved slowly onward in a stooping position, keeping my gun as a battery in front; behind me walked an English *setter*, who, being useless for partridge shooting, I was training for the nobler sport.

" The light hardly penetrated the dense jungle, so that I could not distinguish my companion through the gloom, although I heard him advancing as cautiously as myself.

" At length I got within about fifteen paces of the spot where the dog was giving tongue. I knew I was in an exposed position, but could not avoid it; being unable to move to the right or left, the brambles were so thickly matted together. *Merkis*, encouraged by my presence, ran to and fro yelping bravely: but searched in vain to get a sight of the enemy.

" ' Can you see him?' said the son of America, who was some yards to my left.

" ' Hush!' I replied, for at that moment I fancied I could hear the beast move. My setter also now pricked up his ears and rushed forward. It was the affair of an instant, for hardly had I fixed my gun to my shoulder when I saw *Cato* pushed forward by the boar, and howling with fright.

" It was useless to fire; for such was their position, that I should have killed the dog without hurting the boar. But the difficulty was soon removed: for the boar, throwing the dog behind him, at once was on the muzzle of my gun. I pulled both triggers; but the very instant that I fired, my gun was dashed from my hand; and I and the enraged animal rolled together on the ground. I was undermost, and managed to keep my face downwards to the earth, lying as flat and as still as possible. The path of the boar being, happily for me, a small watercourse, had been worn away; so that the shallow trench somewhat protected me from its tusks. Having recovered from the shots, the monster began to belabour me with his snout; but, being a little flurried, I suppose, could not manage to get a rip. I was in a terrible fright, and hallooed for assistance, expecting every moment to be in the same plight as poor *Zeitsoon*, whose dreadful wound flashed across my mind.

" My companion had now come up boldly to the rescue. ' Take care,' cried I, ' you don't put a ball into me.' *Bang, bang*, went both barrels. The boar left me, and made at his new assailant, who, keeping his gun steady, and having the advantage of being in the thicket, was preserved from the awkward accident which had happened to myself. *Merkis*, seeing him in danger, had boldly laid hold of the boar behind; and Cato was mustering courage, like myself, to assist him; when the boar, worried by *Merkis*, shook him from his hold, and turned after the dogs. Cato was again wounded.

" Having recovered my gun, which by the blow of his snout had been thrown from my hand, I requested my companion to examine me, and see whether I was injured, for I was covered with blood, and whether it was the boar's or mine I could not say, so completely had fear taken away all sense of pain.

" ' Load your gun,' was his cool reply; ' and then we will see what is the matter.'

" We now heard the hunters shouting to us from outside the wood to abandon the boar; that they were certain he was a *Jin*, and that we should both of us be killed or receive some dreadful wound.

" The dogs were giving tongue at some distance ahead of us, and again Sharky shouted—' God is great! Get out, you black *Jin*.'

" ' Come,' said my cool friend, having examined me and found I was only marked by the snout and hoofs of the pig, ' I calculate we will fix him this time. Let us keep together, however, and it is my turn to go first. Finding that I was not quite killed, and roused by the tongue of the dogs, I again dashed onward with him into the thicket.

" ' Do you see him ? ' said I, as we approached the dogs.

" ' Yes,' he whispered; ' make yourself easy, he is coming towards us.' I grasped my gun, and stooping abreast with him in the path, we awaited our foe's assault. He was white with age. Blood was streaming down his side. He did not appear to see us; but was watching the dogs.

" ' Now,' cried I, ' four barrels at once, and I think we can kill even a *Jin*.'

" We fired—the boar fell, got up, staggered, and again rushed gallantly towards us.

" The branches which we clung to for safety barely sustained our weight. My companion, who is a larger man than myself, sometimes swung as low as the snout of the boar.

" *Merkis* again called off the animal's attention, giving a sly snap, and then retreating. The boar moved from us a few paces, and we ventured to quit our trees. I had no balls left: my companion had but one, which he now fired, having put the muzzle of his gun almost on the animal's head, who, though much weakened from loss of blood, was still standing gallantly. As the son of America fired, the beast sank on his hind legs.

" We drew our knives, and, assassin-like, stole behind him. Fierce even in death, he tore with his teeth the bushes near him. Foam and blood gushed from his mouth. As we advanced he made a fresh effort; but at the same moment our hunting-knives were plunged in his heart.

" ' Who-op, who-op,' we cried; ' the devil is dead!' *Merkis* said something to the same purpose. Poor fellow, he had received an ugly rip in the neck. We found every shot that was fired had entered the body of the boar. The carcass bore eleven marks of our balls.

" We had great trouble to drag the bulky brute into the open field. He measured six feet four inches from snout to tail, and three feet three inches from shoulder to hoof, and, though not fat, weighed above twenty stone. However, lean as he was, he yielded us some capital chops.

" Poor *Zeitsoon* was carried home; but never recovered his wounds, though he lingered many days."

" There is no strength nor power but in God!" cried my audience.

After a pause, an old fellow, who had until now been quite silent, pushed off the hood of his gelab, and looking earnestly at me, asked if I was not the Nazarene who had killed the *Melon Boar*?

" Yes," I replied, " I am he."

" Come, then," said the lion-hunter, " you owe me still another tale; for I have told you two."

" The play is fair," said I; " and the story shall be told."

" The *Melon Boar*, then, I must apprise you, was the largest beast of the kind I ever saw; and he was reported to be committing great devastation on some melon-fields in the wood of *Belayashee*.

" I and our fellow-hunter, Ali Sefer, sallied out to try our luck.

" On arriving at the field, a little before sunset, we found the

owners with a pack of curs preparing to bivouac, for the purpose of scaring away the boar; and they told us, it was no use
firing at him, for there was not a huntsman of any fame in the
neighbourhood who had not had a shot, but without success.
It was, they said, as much as they could do to prevent the beast
destroying all the melons, as he cared little for either dogs or
men : nay, he would stay quietly at the border of the wood, until
he found an occasion for rushing in to seize a melon, with which
he would make off into the thicket; and when dogs and men
were tired with watching and overcome by sleep, he would
boldly enter the ground and bite, as if for mere spite, a piece
out of every melon that was fit to eat. In fact, they thought
him to be some evil-disposed *Jin*, and therefore it might be even
an unholy act to kill him; for there was no knowing, some
whispered, what might happen in such a case.

" ' Well,' said I, ' let me try my hand, and if I fail as others
have done, I will pay for every melon he destroys : but I hope
for success; for we Nazarenes, you know, have ourselves
something of the *Jin* about us: and when *Jin* meets *Jin*, the
chances must be nearly equal.'

" ' *Allah Akbar*,' said one of the melon-growers : ' if,
Christian, you only saw his tusks, and how he puts up his bristles
when he enters the field, you would wish yourself in Tangier
again ! ' ' But come,' said they, ' let us place the Nazarene, for
the sun is nearly set, and you may be certain the boar is now
listening to all we are saying.'

" I was now conducted to a pomegranate bush, near which
there were some ripe melons. Here I was to station myself;
and by squatting cross-legged on the ground, I was partly hidden
by some long grass. Ali Sefer wished to be my companion,
but I preferred, as I always do at night-hunts, to be alone, being
thus more likely to keep awake.

" ' May God preserve you,' said the party as they took their
leave; ' and take care,' they added, ' not to sleep. We shall
be within hearing of your shot, and will come to your assistance
the moment you fire.'

" ' Well, good night,' I replied : and I now put on my hooded
gelab, and having rolled a bit of white paper round the muzzle
of my gun, I settled myself in the best position for my bivouac.

" The sound of the Moors' footsteps had scarcely died away, when a slight *crackling* in the wood drew my attention; and soon I heard, and plainly, the rooting and the footsteps of some large animal.

" ' At any rate,' thought I, ' he does not move like a supernatural being.' Whilst I was waiting in this state of excitement for the boar's approach, I heard the tread of a man's foot in a different direction from that by which the party had retired; and shortly I saw a long gun-barrel glisten in the twilight, over the hedge. When the man who carried it reached the low gate, and had cautiously thrown it open, he peered into the field; and then, to my surprise, and some fear too, he levelled his long barrel exactly at the spot where I was sitting. In a moment I cocked my own gun, and pointing it at his head, called out in Arabic—' Who is there?'

" ' Your better,' was his reply.

" ' That,' I retorted, ' remains to be proved. Down with your gun, or I fire!'

" ' Son of the English,' said the hunter, who recognised my voice, ' thank God! I did not fire; but you looked so very like a boar, as you sat under the pomegranate bush, that I was just going to pull the trigger when you called out.'

" ' I fear,' said I to the hunter, who proved to be no other than my friend Hadj Abdallah, ' you have spoiled my sport, for the boar will have made off.'

" ' No, no,' he said, ' I have fired at this boar half a dozen times in the same night: he is now listening to what we are saying; and when we have ceased to make a noise, he will come in for his melon just as if nobody was here, and carry it off to the wood.'

" I now begged the Hadj to join the rest of the party, for I wished to be alone, and accordingly he took his leave.

" The last rays of daylight had now disappeared; the night was cold; there was no moon; and the stars, usually bright in your climate, were dimmed by clouds : the wood began to echo with the howlings of jackals, and the squalling of the genet and ichneumon, searching for their prey : and soon the dull sound f the evening-gun at Gibraltar came booming to my ears, and old it was nine o'clock. I had given up all hope of the boar returning, when a dark shadow passed rapidly across the field, and, retreating to the wood, rather startled me. I then heard the munching of a melon. 'That was cleverly done,' thought I, 'and Jin-like; but try such a manoeuvre again, my fine fellow, and I will be your match.'

"Some minutes elapsed, and again the same dark shadow passed, stopped for a moment, and then made towards the wood. I determined, however, not to fire till I could get a near shot; and I thought that, perhaps, the animal hearing no noise, would be less rapid in his movements. Again and again the same thing occurred; and I was counting the number of melons he would manage to destroy before the morning, and which I should have to pay for, when the boar, entering as before, stopped, and began to blow, and make the low moan which you Moors interpret 'I hope there is no treachery.' I aimed my gun at his head, which was towards me; but he was too far off for me to fire at him in a dark night. Taking courage on finding no dog to molest him, he began to root quite at his ease, and gradually neared the spot where I was posted, till he came within twenty paces.

"I held my breath, and cocked my gun; his whole side was turned towards me: I aimed at his shoulder, I then lowered my gun to be sure that my aim was good; again I pointed, again I lowered it; a third time I levelled, pulled both triggers at once, and threw myself flat on my face. I heard the beast rush by me, and, as it appeared to me, fall some twenty yards beyond: there was a slight kicking for a few moments, and then all was quiet. Still lying on the ground, I quietly loaded my gun, and half raised myself to see if I could make him out.

"The owners of the field and Ali Sefer soon joined me. I told them what I had done, but they would not believe that the animal was wounded.

"'Take care,' said I, 'of yourselves; for he may be on the top of us before we are aware.'

"'Where,' said one of them, 'did you hear him last?'

"I led the man to the spot among some long grass.

"'There ought to be blood hereabouts, then, if the animal is wounded,' said he, putting down his hand. As he did this he started back, and ran off shouting ' E'Sheetan, E'Sheetan.'* I put the muzzle of my gun down, and found that there was the boar, but the beast was already quite dead.

" They would hardly credit my success at first: but when they discovered the monster to be truly dead, they were most eloquent in their praises.

" ' May God make you a true believer,' was their shout, ' for you have no equal.'

" As the morning dawned, it showed my game to have been a very powerful animal, and excessively 'fat with his good living.

" When I bade adieu to my honest friends the melon-growers, they obliged me to accept a present of their excellent fruit, as a reward for having destroyed the robber *Jin.*"

* The Devil—the Devil.

CHAPTER IV.

Proceed on our Journey—River Kholj—Its Inhabitants—Pass of Garbeea—
Scene at a Well—Partridges—River of Mills—Village of Ammar—Mona
—Horse Fight—Economy of Arab Tent—A Visit to the Ladies—Pop the
Question—Introduction to a Harem—Description of the Interior—Lose
my Heart—Estimate of Female Beauty.

My party being ready for a start, we bade our friends the hunters
good sport, and proceeded on our journey.

We soon obtained a fine view of the coast, as far as the ancient town of Azyla, and the surf of the Atlantic was visible, as
we overlooked the sand-hills which formed the long line of
coast.

Our path, as we descended the hill, was like a staircase; so,
for safety, we gave our nags their heads, trusting entirely to
their cautious treading. Having reached the bottom of the hill,
we pursued our course through a plain about two miles broad,
of the richest alluvial soil, patched here and there by fine crops
of drà and maize. In the rainy season this flat land is covered
with water, some two feet deep; and then it swarms with water-
fowl, amongst which are sometimes seen the lady-like Numidian
crane and flocks of the stately flamingo, looking at a distance,
with their scarlet wings, like a troop of British soldiery.

The river *Kholj* meanders through the plain; it is a dangerous torrent in the winter, and many a man and beast have
found a watery grave in it, though now it scarcely reached our
horses' knees.

The Hadj, who had travelled in the East, and had seen the
crocodile of the Nile, and therefore should be good authority,
told me that a courier swimming across this stream had his arm
torn off by one of those monsters. But although there is a
vague opinion among the people of this country that the crocodile is an inhabitant of some of their rivers, I suspect the Hadj
was mistaken, and that a shark was the malefactor.

Reaching the southern side of the plain, we ascended the pass of *Garbeea.* The soil of this upland is a red sand, in which I noticed a considerable variety of fossil shells, some of great beauty.

An ancient well on the side of our track up the hill drew my attention. A very pretty Arab girl stood by it, having in one hand a pitcher of such classic form as would have done credit to the ancient potters of Etruria; whilst in the other she held a small goat-skin, which she was so busied in filling that she let fall her veil of striped cotton, and displayed her *sacred* features to the unhallowed gaze of the *infidel.* A few wild olive-trees overhung the spot, and completed a very pretty picture.

A large tribe of Arabs, the *Oolad Sebaita,* dwell in this district, being nomad within its extent, as is the case with all that race throughout North Africa; and the sons of *Sebaita* were now encamped on the top of the hill, which forms here the left bank of the basin of *Al Kholj.* Palmettos and furze were, at this dry season, almost the only objects that parched nature presented in a garb of green, and seemed to be the only vegetation which the herds and flocks could now find to browse on.

We pursued our way through scattered fields of the stubble of fine wheat and barley, which showed, what indeed the traveller cannot fail to observe throughout the whole of West Barbary, that it wants but a good government, encouraging industry and fostering the people's comfort, to make its wide extent, more than half of which is now as neglected as the desert, one vast garden, producing alternately in its hills and valleys the agricultural wealth of the north of Europe and the tropics.

Our path literally swarmed with partridges, and, having my gun, I blazed away unmercifully; for, unlike their persecuted tribe in the neighbourhood of Tangier, they would not rise, but continued running vexatiously at a short distance in front of me, till I was constrained, in unsportsmanlike fashion, to fire at them on the ground, when I laid low about half a covey at a shot.

One would have fancied I was about to attack some dread beast, for the Hadj kept close in my rear, prepared with a formidable knife, and waiting the effect of my shot, when he would rush forward and cut the throats of the victims, while he turned them towards the tomb of his prophet, pronouncing the " *Bismillah* "* ere the last struggles were past. Some fine birds he picked up; but as life appeared extinct, he again dropped them in distress. It was one of Mohamed's, or rather Moses's, wise ordinances to prevent cruelty in the mode of putting animals to death, that if the knife be blunt, or the smallest notch be found visible after its use, the animal is declared unlawful food. There is, however, some dispute amongst the doctors of Islam, whether what is killed in the chace is not lawful even if it die before the hunter reaches it, provided, on charging the missile, he has pronounced " Bismillah."

In the ardour of the sport, our whole party had wandered from the proper track, and we were now trudging on in a direction which would have led us to Alcassar, when a shepherd, with the quick intelligence and benevolent courtesy that are often found among the children of nature in this country, divining our error, hallooed at the top of his voice from a great distance, and brought us back to the right road.

About four in the evening we reached a beautiful valley, through which ran a clear stream, called the River of Mills; the ruins of several of which are crumbling on its banks, as I have observed to be the case in other parts of this country,— sorrowful evidence that this important engine has dropped into disuse amongst these barbarians of the nineteenth century. Here the nags were watered, as we were approaching the place of our encampment for the night, where there would not be such means of quenching their thirst.

On reaching the summit of the opposite side of the valley, we were cheered by a view of the tents of the wealthy Sheikh Hadj Caoocm, which lay before us distant about an hour's journey.

On approaching the dwelling of the sheikh, who, under the Basha of the northern province, is himself Hakkem, or governor, over a district some thirty miles in breadth, we passed through a large Arab village named Ammar, signifying in Arabic " the cultivated," or " the colonized." Troops of sun-burnt children, some completely naked, and packs of various kinds of dogs,

* In the name of God.

screeched and howled at our strange appearance as we passed
Between five and six o'clock we came to a halt, when the Mallem was dispatched to announce our arrival with many salams,
and to ask permission to pitch our tent for the night near those
of the Hakkem for better security.

Hadj Cassem was indisposed; but as soon as he heard of our
arrival, he sent his principal *saheb*, or follower, to bid us welcome, and to express his regret that he was prevented by illness
from saluting us in person. He requested me to order whatever
I required, and to pitch my tent on the right of his own, which
we did immediately, assisted by the Saheb Kaid Alarby, who
was brother-in-law to the Hakkem, and whom we soon found a
jovial trifler with the tenets of his prophet.

We had scarcely pitched our tents, when four men presented
themselves, bearing a mona* of sheep, fowls, barley, &c., which
were laid at our feet on the part of the Hakkem as a provision
for the night, and enough there was for five times the number
of our little party. One of the bearers, who acted as spokes-
man, bawled out " that this was only a small token of his lord's
esteem for the British, whom he regarded as the most honest of
the Room (Europeans), and well deserving the Moslem's esteem,
having always been their best ally." I called the Saheb Kaid
Alarby aside, and, having expressed to him how sensibly I felt
the friendship of his chief, I intimated that, being unprovided
with a gift on my own part, it was out of my power to receive
such liberal *mona*, but I ventured to say I should be happy to
pay its value.

"Do you call this a present?" exclaimed Alarby; " if the
Hakkem had sent you a horse or a couple of cows, you might
then talk about making some return. You are here as 'the
guests of God,' and as such must be provided for. If you refuse
the mona, not a man in the village dare sell or give you a crumb
of bread; and it is not to you only that we do this, but to every
one. Even now," he continued, "a miserable infidel of a Jew
arrived here, and a mona of bread and a fowl was sent him by
our lord."

* A gift of food for travellers, of which the name is supposed to have its
origin in that of *manna*, the miraculous provision bestowed by the bounty of
Heaven on the Israelites while wandering in the deserts of Arabia.

Finding all opposition useless, I accepted the offering with a good grace ; and, giving a trifle to each of the bearers, returned our thanks to the Kaid for his hospitality, the fame of which, I added, with a true Arabic flourish, was spread from east to west and from north to south, among Moslem, Christian, Jew, and Pagan.

We now retired to our tent, and having performed our ablutions and donned the dressing-gown and slippers, a comfortable deshabille at this season, we each of us surmounted the loose costume with a lady's bonnet and veil, the most approved mosquito curtain for the narrow compass of a tent, and with which we were provided by fair hands in Tangier, to guard us against those insects, which begin their detestable attacks towards evening.

The Saheb Alarby, hearing that I was on the look-out for a horse, now came to the tent to inform me that he had ordered the best in the village to be brought for my inspection. I accordingly sallied out in my strange costume, and was greeted with much less surprise and ridicule on the part of the Arabs than I should have been in my proper garb of a Christian man. In fact, my party-coloured dressing-gown gained the admiration of many, and as for my head-dress, one young urchin observed, after some deliberation, that it would be capital gear for robbing a bee-hive in.

Several fine barb stallions, held by the Hakkem's slaves, were led forward, amongst which was a powerful black colt, who, having managed, by rearing and plunging, to break loose from his conductor, attacked, with thrown back ears, open mouth, and tail erect, another of the stud ; and, notwithstanding all the efforts of the Arabs, accustomed to such freaks, a desperate fight ensued, —wheeling round as quick as lightning, rearing, and using their fore feet as dexterously as an expert boxer ; then galloping away from those who endeavoured to catch them, determined to have out their duel, snorting and squealing most wildly. This was a moment for the admirers of horse-flesh to see every muscle and nerve come into play in their fine action unrestrained :—

> " Imperiously he leaps, he neighs, he bounds,
> And now his woven girts he breaks asunder ;
> His ears uppricked, his braided hanging mane
> Upon his compass'd crest now stands on end ;
> His nostrils drink the air, and forth again

As from a furnace vapours doth he send ;
His eye, which glistens scornfully like fire,
Shows his hot courage and his hot desire." *

The black colt was at length seized by the neck by his more vigorous adversary, who, pressing him to the ground, held him there till men came to the rescue, and separated the combatants.

Previous to our return to the tent, we took a stroll, accompanied by the Saheb Alarby, through the village. The winter residence of the Hakkem was an oblong building, constructed of large sun-dried bricks ; it had a flat terrace, was without windows, and a considerable portion of it was partitioned off as a pen for the cattle.

His tents, in which he chiefly resides during summer, had an appearance of comfort, being of the same class as the larger military tent used by superior officers in Marocco.

These tents are very different from those in common use with us : their walls are for the most part made of stout hempen cloth, but even those of a very considerable size have only one pole, which is generally square, and divided in two pieces ; it is of great strength, and placed in the centre. The arrangement of the cords is perhaps better adapted for expedition in pitching than our own. All the cords, being brought together, are attached to a longer one, which is fastened to a peg driven into the ground some twenty yards distant. The exterior is varied with figures cut in blue cloth to resemble what is commonly called the " bearded parapets." A large globe surmounted by a javelin-point adorns the top.

The interior is lined according to the wealth of its owner, the material being sometimes strong silk or fine damask. I remember seeing the tent of an important personage, the governor of a province, which had been a gift from the sultan. It was very large, resembling in form the marquee of a European officer of high rank, and was formed within and without of fine broadcloth of brilliant scarlet and sky-blue. Mats, carpets, and cushions are the usual furniture of the tent, as they are of the houses in the towns.

The tents of the Arabs have a very different aspect, being of a

* Shakspeare.

black or brown stuff made of the palmetto fibre, of goats' hair or camels' wool, of each of which materials the natives form very strong webs for this purpose.   They are supported by two poles, with a traverse bar connecting them at top to sustain the roof. These tents are seldom more than seven or eight feet high in the centre, but in length from twenty to thirty feet, and with some wealthy sheikhs they are considerably larger.   Their form is somewhat similar to that of a boat with its keel upwards.   The sides of the tent are, in the colder seasons of the year, pinned to the ground, but in the summer are so arranged as to leave a foot or more of space all round for ventilation ; and the seclusion of the inhabitants is effected by a light hedging of some dry bushes, and often of withered plants of the *onopordon macrocanthum*, a splendid thistle that adorns the rich and neglected soil of North. Marocco.   From the free ventilation thus simply obtained, the Arab tents are far more cool in summer, and, probably, warmer in winter, than the more luxurious-looking houses of the Moors, who dwell in towns.

. The tent-cloth is woven with such peculiar skill as to resist the penetration of wet, although, during both " the former and the latter rain," the clouds pour out their bounty as copiously as they did for " the chosen people in Judea," and, during the latter season, as heavily sometimes as within the tropics.

A simple reed-mat is spread as a floor, over which the wealthy lay a goats'-hair carpet.   Every family has its brood of chickens, and these have their roosting quarter in a distant nook or compartment of the tent.

In one corner is to be seen the primitive hand-mill, which may at once be described by saying that it is in all respects the same simple machine that has been used from time immemorial by the inhabitants of our British Isles, and is yet to be seen as the quern of Scotland ;—and the biblical reader, on seeing it worked by the women of West Barbary, will be reminded of the doom prophesied in the Gospel, " Two women shall be grinding at the mill ; the one shall be taken and the other left."*

The millstones used throughout a great part of Al-gharb are cut from a vast cave about a mile and a half south of Cape

* Matthew xxiv. 41.

Spartel, which, from the considerable extent it has been worked
for this and other purposes, seems to indicate a quarry of very
great antiquity. And indeed I am led to believe that the cave
sacred to Hercules, as recorded by Mela, was situated at this very
spot. *

But to return to the interior of the Arab's tent : one sees near
the quern two earthen slabs, between which they bake flat cakes
of wheaten flour, or of barley, drà, or maize ; all which are
agreeable food when fresh. Their wheat and barley cakes are
very like our Scots skons and bannocks both in taste and
appearance.

In another place is seen the spinning-wheel and distaff, and a
loom also ; all these implements are evidently of the earliest
forms, and are probably identically those of the days of Abraham.
A large and grotesque-fashioned chest, painted in a rude but not
inelegant Arabesque tracery of red, white, and blue colouring,
with a few earthern jars, a saddle, and a long gun, complete the
furniture of the Arab's home.

During the day their scanty couches are suspended like ham-
mocks from the roof pole, thus allowing a freer space to the
women in their domestic employments.

As we passed through the dooar, women and children flocked
to the doors of the tents to have a sight of the Nazarene. I remarked amongst them a tall and aged dame, round whose neck
was tattooed the representation of a chain, with the cross of Christ
suspended to it. She perhaps could trace her descent from some
tribe which had been tributary to the Roman colonists, who first
planted the Christian church in these regions. Hence it may be
inferred, that what under the empire of Rome and Byzantium
was a needful token for security to the pagans, is yet retained by
these close adherents to ancient usage ; although the faith of their
masters has been for ages changed, and not only has the necessity
for the talisman ceased, but even its origin is forgotten amongst
them.

There are several curious relics of Romish devotion still in use
amongst them. The following, I am assured, is very generally

---

* These excavations extend for a considerable distance into the sea ; and
traces of quarrying are in many places clearly discernible several feet below
the present *low-water* mark.

observed :—Should a woman in travail be in danger, the midwife
and female friends assemble round her, and, waving white kerchiefs, implore the Virgin Mary to come to the assistance of the
sufferer, saying, " O Mareea, Mareea, come, come :—delay not,
O thou blessed one ; come to the help of this woman in danger,"
&c.　When the woman is delivered, a like ceremony takes place
to facilitate the return of the Virgin Mary to paradise.

The tattooed old lady, advancing frankly towards our party,
invited us to visit her tent, upon which, as we found the Saheb
did not oppose our accepting her hospitality, we followed her,
whilst Kaid Alarby kept aloof; for, as he was known to be a sad
rake, his approaching the women would have stirred up the demon
of jealousy among their lords.

The country folk in Marocco, it may be observed by the way,
are far less jealous for their women's virtue than those in the
towns—a pleasing evidence this of better principles springing
out of the more simple life.

On entering the tent, we were surrounded by a female host;
and it was vastly amusing to observe the strange effect we pro-
duced among them.　Some showed fear ; some cursed us ; some
admired the whiteness of our skin, which, by the bye, was already
tanned deeper than nut-brown ; others would touch us, and then
leap back and laugh outright.

There was not much pretension to beauty amongst them ; their
large black and hawk-like eyes, softened by the long silken eye-
lash, being in our opinion their only redeeming feature.

Our Arab hostess now handed us an ample bowl of milk, of
which we partook ; and, returning our thanks, I gained the good
graces of all our coterie of charmers by addressing the following
Arabic couplet to them :—

" My thoughts are perplexed.　How can I describe your beauty !
Whether to compare it with the sun, the moon, or wandering star !
Snow and fire are in your cheeks assembled.
How wonderful is this union between the fire and snow !"

These were the first Arabic words I had spoken ; and there
was a general burst of acclamation—" He is Arby, he is Arby !"
[an Arab].　Then followed a thousand questions ; but, having
accidentally pulled off my glove, the clatter of tongues ceased at
once, and all shrunk back in horror at what they considered an

act of sorcery, looking aghast, and seeming to mutter in alarm, " What next! " reminding me of the old story of the frog whose tail dropped off.

" O most merciful God! " the old woman exclaimed, " keep us from Jins, and from men that work by the evil spirit."

It cost me some trouble before I could prevail on any of them to feel the glove and be assured that it was not an outer skin of my own limb. Their confidence being after awhile regained, I was asked if the Nazarene women were pretty, and how many wives I had; and " Can Christian women," said one little girl, putting forward her hands, which were highly dyed with henna, " paint their hands like mine?"

" No, in truth," I replied, " and that is partly the reason I am not yet married; but I have long been in search of a pretty wife, and now I am willing to contract for any one, or two, or even three of the gazelles around me; and," added I, " a dower of camels, oxen, sheep, and everything else shall be given in treble the quantity that would be offered by one of your own race." Every brown face of young and old was now put forward, calling on me to choose.

" You are all beautiful," I exclaimed; " but the hospitality of my hostess has won my entire heart."

The younger of the assemblage were half amused, half vexed, on hearing me thus, with a serious countenance, select for my bride the gaunt old mistress of the tent.

This scene reminds me of a visit I had once the rare luck to make to the harem of a great man in this curious country.

Having passed the outer porch of the Cid's abode through a low arch of horseshoe form, the party of which I was one were conducted into a little garden, where the verbena-louisa, the jessamine, and the rose vied in luxuriant vegetation. Our path was shaded from the piercing rays of a September sun by the thick foliage of vines trained over fantastic trellises of cane, through which hung temptingly within our reach fine grapes, both red and white, with some of a singular ash-colour, and others of a long tapering form, peculiar perhaps to this country, and called, in the poetical language of the people's Arab ancestry, " the damsel's fingers."

We ascended a few steps to an alcove, in front of which played a bubbling fountain, and through its jet of sparkling water came the cool breeze scented by flowers. Here we found our host sitting on a rich Rabat carpet, in the cross-legged tailor fashion universal in this country, with many an embroidered cushion to complete the luxury of his divan.

A little behind the great man, yet where he could wait and watch for every wish of his lord, stood a young bronze-coloured slave, whose fine eyes rolled their white orbs in astonishment at the Nazarene visitors.

Three handsomely carved chairs had been placed for the Christians; such chairs as one might suppose to have been a gift to an ancestor of the kaid from some friendly governor of Tangier in the time of our merry King Charles.

"You are welcome," said our host, as we entered the alcove, and accompanied his salutation with a mechanical counting on his rosary of green ivory beads. "You are welcome—God knows I have long wished for this visit." Then followed a succession of compliments, which we returned with compound interest. After a time he nodded to the slave, who, opening a side door, ushered in several attendants, the first of whom bore a polished brass tray, on which was arranged a vast bowl of the finest sugar in very large lumps, with a teapot and diminutive cups of delicate porcelain; the others followed, bearing pyramids of cakes and sweetmeats, all of which having been placed before us on little stands of carved wood, painted and gilded in Arabesque, they bowed and retired.

We were now to be drenched with tea; for, like the pipe in Turkey, at all hours of the day must a guest submit to be regaled with this watery beverage; and three times, alas! were our cups to be drained of their over-sweet contents; for the Moor never thinks his drink too sweet, and we well knew that declining any portion would be taken as a slight.

We were rising to take leave, when our host begged us to be seated, saying he would not let us go away without evincing the strongest evidence of his regard for us: "And I have been considering," said he, "what might be most agreeable to you, and I think," and here he drew out a massive key from his girdle, "I think I have hit upon it. You shall see my harem, into which no man has ever entered, not even my own sons since their boyhood. Although my domestic establishment is not to be compared to the luxury of your houses, the curiosity of a European may be gratified by seeing it; for you are ever searching for the strange and marvellous, and your industry has been justly rewarded; for you Room (Romans) have penetrated the mysteries of every science, and have found, by your indefatigable pursuit of human learning, a remedy for every ill to which mortal men are subject, except one—death, the inevitable doom of Moslem and of all!"

He rose, and thrust the key into an ingenious-looking lock. "These," said he, "are the apartments of my last lala, whom our lord the sultan—God prolong his life, and make happy his existence!—has lately presented to me; and, as the ladies are apt to quarrel with any rival in the affections of their master, I have lately built these rooms for her reception."

Such presents, by the way, are common in this country from the Moorish potentate to his favoured officers; but, thought I, as I crossed the sacred threshold, this must be a hazardous present to receive: the fair one, relieved from the duties of the court, may be difficult to please in the humbler mansion.

The habitation of the favourite consisted of a court-yard open to the sky, with a room on each side; a fountain played in the centre, and in one quarter there was a vapour-bath. The floor and sides of the court were prettily laid in coloured tiles, bordered with precepts from the Koran. The folding-doors which opened into the principal dormitory were beautifully carved in intricate mathematical figures, and the walls were richly decorated in Arabesque stucco-work: fine velvet couches and cushions of embroidered leather were ranged around the room; and opposite the door, on an elaborately painted rack, hung a fine Algerine gun, the barrel of which was curiously damascened with gold, and the stock inlaid with coral and silver: below it was suspended a clumsy Moorish sword in a scabbard of gold and velvet; this weapon was also a gift of his Shereefian majesty.

The ceiling was adorned with minute mouldings richly painted and gilded, and of the same intricate devices as are yet to be seen in the Alhambra of the Caliphat in Grenada.

At one end of the room stood the trousseau-box of a bride, made of the famous pine of the Moorish highlands, called

L'Aris; it was elegantly carved in Saracenic fashion, and from the fine perfume of the timber must, I should suppose, be well adapted for the preservation of apparel. On this box I noticed an eight-stringed lute and the noisy *tomtom*.

Thence we passed into a large court ornamented with slender pillars of white marble; and through rooms hung with damask, and furnished with carpets of the finest colours, and much thicker than the best of those from Turkey.

Instead of pictures, which are all proscribed in Islam, hung the old-fashioned German mirrors in large and newly-gilded frames; but I started on looking into one of them, for I found my face so absurdly distorted in the wavy glass, that I had well nigh spoiled all my courtesies by a hoarse laugh.

A brass frame, in the shape of two intersecting squares, served as a chandelier in the centre of the ceiling of each room. These brazen frames are sometimes composed of two intersecting equilateral triangles, and this latter appears to be the correct form of a symbol which is held sacred by several races in the East, under the name of Solomon's seal.

The only apertures for light and air to these apartments, when the doors are shut, are worked in plaster, seeming almost as delicate as filagree; they fill several niches in the form of what we call "Gothic windows;" and of these there were three or four over each doorway; there was, however, one small chamber in the second story, out of harm's way, which had two tolerably sized windows, closely latticed however, whence the prisoned inmates of the harem might unseen feast their eyes on a valley of orange and citron plantations, which border a serpentine stream named "Boosafa" (the Father of Clearness). This beautiful stream runs rapidly from its inexhaustible sources in the rugged pile of mountains that overhang the city, whose name of *Tetouan* indicates, in the Berber tongue, its many fountains.

Whilst our host was noting to my companions the names of the villages that are to be seen from a lattice, through which they were admiring the distant scene, I became impatient at a nomenclature which I had already by heart, and so moved sauntering away, peering about into sundry curious nooks and passages that form the strange distribution of a Moorish palace. At length, becoming somewhat alarmed at my own hardihood,

E

I turned to rejoin the master of the house; when a door, through the chinks of which all my movements must have been watched, was thrown open, and out rushed the Houris, black, white, half-caste, fat, thin, old, and young! It was impossible for me to escape, and had I made a precipitate movement, I should have become liable to the worst of imputations; so I stood stock still, and was quickly arrested by the powerful paws of a jet-black dame, and then commenced a general scrutiny of my person.

"Look," said one, "I told you the Nazarenes had a mouth, and a nose, and ears, just like Mohamedans!"

"See," said another, taking up my hand; "one, two, three, four, five!!—exactly the same number!"

"But what are these?" screamed a third, who had laid hold of the skirts of my coat; "does he hide his tails here?"

"And he laughs, too!" they exclaimed.

From this, indeed, I could no longer refrain, although I was becoming seriously uneasy lest my absence should be discovered by the great man; for I was now in the midst of the most forbidden fruit, although it proved far inferior to what my fertile fancy had previously imagined. Indeed a less attractive posse of womankind I never beheld; for almost all these ladies were at a time of life when the fineness of the Moorish features had disappeared; and the only redeeming grace that remained to them, which is common, indeed, to all the white women of West Barbary, was the large gazelle eye. As to the admired *en bon point* of youth, it had been replaced by a gross fatness, which smothered forms that were once perhaps of perfect symmetry. According to the taste of the Moor, a lady is in perfection when her charms are a load for a camel.

One, however, of this motley circle deserved all my admiration as a Mauritanian Venus. This was a delicate-looking girl; her age, I thought, was sweet fifteen—the prime of womanhood in this precocious country; for their beauty seems to fade with the *teens*. Her complexion was very fair, her eyes dark hazel, to which the black border of " Kohol " * gave a languid expression. She had a coral-lipped mouth, round as a ring, as the Moorish ode describes the feature.† Her black hair, braided

* Antimony,
† See the Moorish ode at the end of the volume.

with silver cords, waved in profusion over her shoulders. Her sylph-like figure was clothed in a pale green caftan, embroidered on the bosom and skirt in silver thread. This garment reached a little below her knees, and over it she wore an outer robe of light gauze, confined around the waist by a red zone of Fez silk. The sleeves of her caftan were wide, and open near the wrist; showing at every turn an arm like alabaster, which was encircled by a plain but massive bracelet of Soodan gold; and her uncovered legs were seen from below the caftan clasped with chased silver; her feet were also bare, for in her sally with the rest she had forgotten her slippers; her feet, as well as her hands, were dyed with henna of a bright orange colour. Over her head she had thrown a light muslin kerchief; but in this sudden tumult her curiosity got the better of her national caution, and she stood before me quite unveiled.

During the uproar occasioned by my intrusion, the youthful damsel was the only one silent; but now taking alarm from the noise of the rest, she half hid her pretty features, and cried in an anxious whisper, "Hush! hush! hush! My father will hear; and then, oh! what will become of this young Christian?"

"What do we care?" said a barrel of a woman, with eyes that rolled like gooseberries in a saucer, and whom I took to be the most favoured dame of this party-coloured assemblage; for her dress far surpassed that of all the rest in costliness. "It was the Christian's fault for daring to ——." She could not finish her speech, for the gruff voice of their lord was heard.

"What is that noise? Where's the other Nazarene?" And then his heavy step came tramping nearer and nearer.

Off scampered all the surrounding spirits, black, white, and grey. The little damsel was the last to move, and evidently with less apprehension than the rest. Veiling closely all her features except one dear eye, she said to me, in a quick whisper, "Don't be afraid, Nazarene. Tell my father it was all our fault; he is very good-natured, and you are so young."

I had by luck a rosebud at my breast. I answered by giving it to her with a thanking smile; and instantly she flew after her companions.

"*Ellee Haramy!* Hollo, young rascal!" said the big man, as he laid hold of me by the collar; and I began to feel that my

E 2

head was very insecure on my shoulders. "Kah, kah, kah!" and his fat sides shook with laughter; "So, boy! (my chin was yet smooth) you have been among my women, eh! Don't you know you deserve to die?" suiting the action to the word by drawing his hand across my throat. "Eh! trying to carry off my gazelles! Eh! you young Nazarene."

Though frightened out of my wits, I had just breath enough to gasp out, "O my lord, if I have done anything to displease you, attribute it to ignorance of your customs. In my country it is usual to pay our respects to the ladies in preference to everybody else."

"Ah! deceiver," said he; "you Nazarenes must have a pleasant time of it too. Kah, kah, kah! I must go to your country. Kah, kah! Yes, they speak true; they speak true when they say that your Paradise is on earth. Come along, young sir; I will show you the kitchen, where I have a black beauty in a cook; pay Christian attention to her, if you please. Kah, kah, kah!" And so he led me off, and shortly afterwards we took our leave. In the evening a handsome present was brought me from the great man, which showed that I had not lost his good graces by my audacious visit to his harem.

Here I must present to the reader the Moorish estimate of female beauty, although I am aware that others have given it; for it is found also among the Oriental Arabs, from whom indeed those of Al Gharb derive not only their parentage, but all their more refined ideas, and whatever they retain of poetry in thought and language.

"Four things in a woman should be black—the hair, the eyebrows, the eye-lashes, and the iris of the eyes: four should be white—the complexion, the white of the eyes, the teeth, and legs: four red—the tongue, the lips, the middle of the cheeks, and the gums: four long—the back, the fingers, the arms, and the legs: four round—the head, the neck, the arms, and the ankles: four wide—the forehead, the eyes, the bosom, and the hips: four delicate—the nose, the eyebrows, the lips, and fingers: four ample—the lower part of the back, the thighs, the calves of the legs, and the knees: four small—the ears, the breasts, the hands, and the feet."

CHAPTER V.

Evening Prayers—A Supper—Meet a Lion—Kaid Alarby—Robber's Story
continued—The Sultan—The Champions—The Death-blow—The Spirit
of the Wood.

WHEN the voice of the Mueddin from the tent mosque of the
Doowa announced the prayers of Al Mogreb, or Vespers, we
took leave of our Arab hostess, and joining Kaid Alarby, wended
our way through herds of cattle, flocks of sheep and goats, and
troops of horses, that had already arranged themselves instinc-
tively round the tents of their owners, for security during the
night. My people were now, like all good Mohamedans, prostrating themselves with their faces turned towards the holy
Kaaba; but my honest servant Sharky had, I distinctly observed,
at least one eye directed to the kesksoo pot, which was steaming
with a hopeful odour, and which for my part, I confess, occupied
my whole attention.

During supper the sheikh's son, an intelligent-looking lad of
about twelve years, accompanied by Kaid Alarby, paid us a
visit; and no sooner had we finished our meal, than I was called
upon to make a particular exhibition of our guns, pistols, knives,
saddles, &c., which were all to be severally scrutinized; and, as
the wonders of Christendom worked upon their fancy, prayers
were rapidly muttered in quick succession by all the faithful in
my tent against the wiles of Sheetan (Satan), who is held by
this simple people to reside within the mechanism of our finest
European works, and to regulate their movements.

Such is the ignorance of European art among all classes in
this country, that, some years ago, a resident of Tangier having
in his possession an astronomical telescope which inverted the
objects, and having exhibited it to some Moorish neighbours, it
was bruited about that the Nazarene possessed a glass through
which he looked at the Moorish women on their terraces, and

that this instrument had the power of turning the ladies upside
down! Information was sent to the court, showing the impro-
priety of Christians being allowed to make use of such magic
art; whereupon a mandate was dispatched from the sultan to the
governor of Tangier, directing that the importation of such instruments should be strictly prohibited, and that the Nazarene
who possessed the telescope should be summoned to deliver it up
to the authorities for their examination, and called to account for
his shameless proceeding!

In the meantime the Hadj, the Malem Sharky, and the owner
of the rat-tailed, whom we had all taken a fancy to, and willingly
admitted as one of our party, had managed to dispose beneath
their belts of some half-dozen capons, with a full proportion of
the most satisfying kesksoo. Kaid Alarby left us now to attend
upon another party of travellers, who had just arrived on their
way to Tangier; and who proved to be a kaid and his suite, who
were conducting a lion and lioness, as an imperial present to the
" Sultan" of the United States. But our good friend Alarby,
being somewhat agitated by deep inquiries into a brandy-bottle
which he had discovered in my canteen, reeled his way out of
the tent, making its canvas roof rattle over our heads as he
stumbled amongst the cords, and welcomed the travellers with
his boisterous " Salam oo Alee Koom."

His attachment, however, for myself, or rather for my spirit-
bottle, was not yet exhausted; for he had no sooner disposed of
the comers and their lions, than he came rolling back, praying
loudly for a little more brandy.

" The Hakkem has ordered me," he said, " to superintend
your guards carefully; and to keep out the cold from myself
whilst I am doing so, I must really have a little more of that
Christian medicine."

This I promised to give him, if he would keep strict watch
till the morning outside, and leave us to sleep in peace.

" Hark you, guards!" he now shouted; " hear what I, the
Kaid Alarby, say: I will destroy the house of your fathers if
I find that one single sinner has winked an eye this night!"

Scarcely had he concluded his threat, when we heard his pon-
derous body stumble over the picket of our mule, by whose side
he fell, and slept with her till the dawn, where we then found him.

An hour before sunrise we broke our fast with coffee and kesksoo; and scarcely had the " henna-fingered Aurora " touched the tops of Gibel Habeeb, when, the tents being already struck and the baggage packed, our little party moved off, having first invoked God's blessing on the Hakkem, and bid good bye to jolly Kaid Alarby, who complained of a racking headache, arising—as he told us—from the anxious watch he had kept all night.

For a traveller in this country the early morning is the time of enjoyment; his spirits are then the most elastic; he is refreshed by rest, and braced by the coolness of the balmy air. This delightful feeling can only be estimated by those who have toiled their weary way in a sultry season through a long monotonous tract, within these latitudes.

Having given vent to the overflow of my spirits by a wanton gallop after a hare that started from beneath a palmetto-bush close to our path, I found that our companion of the rat-tailed, with the usual negligence of a Moor, had omitted to secure some of his horse's furniture, and had stopped behind to adjust it. He now came tearing up to me, after his own fashion of Lab-el-barode; and, in the most received style of compliment, fired his gun close to my head.

Having properly acknowledged this compliment, although I was by no means sure that he had not singed my whiskers, I reminded him of his unfinished tale of the robber, and begged him to continue it. He required no second bidding; and, after a complimentary flourish or two in honour of my Nazareneship, thus began :—

" Alee slept soundly after the sultan's supper, though he dreamt of blows.

" ' May God prolong the life of our Lord ! " shouted by thousands of prostrate heads, greeted the Kleefa of the Prophet, the champion of God, as he rode under the imperial umbrella * into the Meshwa, a very spacious court of the palace, where the Father of Islam gives public audience. The monarch was mounted on a snow-white stallion, which, with arched crest

---

* The *D'al*, a very large umbrella, which is in Marocco to this day the ensign of royalty, as it was in very early ages, and still continues to be, in various nations of the East.

and measured steps, moved majestically under his Shereefian burden.

" 'All goes smoothly in the world,' was whispered through the crowd; for thus they interpreted the peaceful colour of the sultan's steed, which is supposed to indicate his sublime highness's humour: for you know, O Nazarene! that white is the symbol of peace and good-will; black, that of hatred and war; chestnut, that of displeasure; whilst the shades of brown, grey, roan, cream-coloured, and the rest, are each known to express the various state of the imperial mind.

" The bridle and head-trappings were superb, being of green silk richly embroidered in gold, whereon was portrayed, easily to be seen by all men, the sacred emblem of Solomon's seal; and in the hollow of the neck might be remarked now and then, through the thick and silvery mane, a small pouch of scarlet leather, wherein was held a portion of the earth of the holy Drees's tomb—upon his soul be peace!—and by its side was suspended, in strange conjunction, the polished tooth of some enormous boar—unholy beast! nevertheless an infallible remedy against the evil eye.

" His saddle, which reposed on a housing of orange damask, was quilted in green, having a poitrel and girths of the stoutest silk, interwoven with gold thread. The ample stirrups were of massive gold, beautifully chased.

" The sultan's simple dress formed a striking contrast with the richness of his horse-furniture. He wore a caftan of white kerseymere, with the Moorish girdle of white leather, embroidered with pale blue silk, fastened by a plain silver buckle. A muslin turban, with the silk tuft of royalty, crowned his imperial head; and over this hung gracefully, in full broad folds, a transparent haik, of the finest fabric of Fas. His legs were equipped in boots of white Marocco leather, curiously worked with devices in silk thread.

" The Meshwa herald now proclaimed that *Shasha* (the blow-giver) and the six-fingered Alee, each of free will, were about to test their strength, and that a royal donation of fifty gold mitzakel* would be the reward of the conqueror.

* A mitzakel is equivalent to about 2s. 6d. sterling.

" ' May God bless our Lord!' shouted by ten times ten thousand voices, drowned the cry of the herald,—' the deafener, as the people called him, from his astounding voice. Both the champions were already on the appointed ground, when there arose the question which should receive the first blow.

" On this the sturdy Alee spoke :—

" ' O mighty Shasha, slave of the Defender of the Faithful, the sultan of the world! it is my duty to grant that advantage even to the meanest servant of our Lord.'

" The Blow-giver replied:

" ' Your course of life is run; it has reached its goal! Where shall I deal the fatal blow?'

" Alee pointed to the top of his head.* The long and muscular arm of the black was now raised and poised in the air over the skull of Alee, who, with knees slightly bent, stood undaunted before his antagonist, a broad grin upon his features, as if certain of his power of resisting all human strength.

" Down came the fist of the black, sounding like the sledge-hammer when struck with force against an anvil. Alee staggered, drops of sweat burst out upon his forehead, his eyes rolled with pain, and seemed starting from their sockets; but recovering, he shook himself, and, rubbing his bullet-shaped head, and looking around, exclaimed: ' Allah! that is what you may call a blow! And what a blow too! Allah! But now comes my turn, O Bokhàry! and if it please the most mighty God, Shasha the blow-giver shall never deal another.'

" Then, turning towards the sultan, he craved to be allowed to place himself on equal height with his tall opponent. This was granted; and four soldiers were ordered to fetch a marble block

---

* With the poorer classes of this country the heads of boys are all closely shaved from their earliest youth, and left bare to the sun or storm, not covered by either cap or turban, and thus the skulls of the rude Moors acquire a thickness as extraordinary as that which historians affirm to have distinguished the ancient Copts.

The Moorish boys when fighting butt against each other with their heads, and he who falls is sure to have the power of his cranium proved by a stone or brick-bat, if one be at hand; and often have I heard such cracks resound upon the Moslem pates as would inevitably have fractured the skull of a hat-wearer, and for the tempting wager of one farthing will many of these lads break you a well-burnt brick over his bare pate with more good will than I would crack a biscuit on my own.

that was at hand, but they found it too much for them. Alee
ran to the spot, and, having with their assistance put it on his
shoulders, brought it and placed it in front of the sultan.

"Then having doffed his gelab, he took his position on the
block, and, clenching his six-fingered fist, and throwing his body
slightly backwards, raised his arm, and seemed to choose a posture whereby he might secure the greatest power. He hesitated,
and dropped his arm, as if to consider a little longer.

"And now the black man trembled, and over his sooty face
there seemed to come a horrid paleness, as Alee resumed, in a
yet more decided manner, his posture of attack.

"Down—rapid as a thunderbolt—fell Alee's fist, and with it
fell the black, never to rise again. The Bokhàry's skull was
frightfully fractured, and he who had so often dealt the blows of
death, was now but as one of those who had met a like fate from
his own relentless arm.

"'There is no power nor strength but in God,' exclaimed
the sultan, as the black expired at his feet. 'Give the clown,'
pointing to Alee, 'the fifty ducats, and let him have safe conduct. Shasha, in truth, is a great loss to my household; but
who can avoid God's decrees, which are written in the Book of
Fate?'

"Alee took the purse; and ere the sultan's mandate for him
to be escorted could be put in force, he had mingled with the
crowd, and was seen no more. Some said that the brethren of
the black murdered him that night."

We all applauded this story, which was especially to the taste
of the Hadj and Mallam Ahmed.

"And was he," said I, "O eloquent follower of the Prophet!
was your thick-skulled hero really slain?"

The owner of the rat-tailed shook his head mysteriously.
"Noble Nazarene," he said, "be it known to you, that not
many weeks after this blow-giving many daring robberies were
reported to have been committed on the highway between Tangier and Tetuan, near Ain Jdeeda (the New Spring), a spot
marked by many a small whitened cairn as a field of blood; also
on the hill of Dar-el-Clow, over which we travelled yesterday;
and in the woods of Sahel near Laraiche, and in the great forest
of Mamòra. No idea could ever be formed as to the number of

the gang, but it was supposed to be numerous, for well-armed kaflas* had shared the same fate as single passengers : and what was the most mysterious, the robbers had never been seen, although some suspected that the marks of cloven feet† in the wild districts where the robberies were committed were those of the marauders.

"Near to the most difficult passes, and from out the darkest and densest thickets, would a deep sepulchral voice threaten the travellers; and the words 'Halt, or you die!' would be heard as uttered close at hand. Should no heed be taken of this command, or should any attempt be made to discover the speaker, as sure as there is another world, a shot would lay low some one of the party. Search or pursuit for these mysterious highwaymen was useless, and often proved the death of many a stout heart. The kaflas and other travellers, finding no resource but to obey this call, came by common consent into a practice of stopping when thus summoned, and according to the demand they deposited on the ground food, clothes, money, or anything which they were commanded to place there by the unseen one, who never failed to accompany his requisition with some dreadful threat if an attempt were made to discover him, or if they delayed making the best of their way off after they had paid the toll.

"Schemes were planned, and ambushes laid for trapping these unknown outlaws, for no one could suppose that the public were the victims of a single robber; but the evil spirit, as the folks firmly believed, thwarted all such attempts, for it seemed the peaceful travellers' enemy had strange foreknowledge of every plot against him, and the fool-hardy adventurers who attempted his capture seldom returned to tell their tale."

* The term used in Marocco for an assemblage of merchants and others travelling with goods, called in the east a karwán, or vulgarly caravan.

† A belief in the fabled satyrs of old Rome yet lingers in the fancy of the people of West Barbary.

CHAPTER VI.

Locusts—Story of the Robber continued—The Taleb—Horrid tale of
Murder—The *Fathá*—The Schoolmaster—The Meeting—Alee's opinions
—The Pass-word—Rahmana—The Capture—Alee in love—The Mar-
riage—The Traitor—The Proclamation.

HE of the " rat-tailed " had proceeded thus far when my Spanish
friend, who had very little knowledge of the Arabic, and had
for a considerable time been groaning in the spirit at the length
of the narrative, interrupted him somewhat abruptly, by calling
my attention to a dense mass of locusts which were busy at their
work of destruction in a field of maize near our path, and which
Don Jose said appeared to him to be of the same species as those
which of late years had infested the plains of La Mancha, and
which the Spaniards had in vain endeavoured to destroy.

We had before met with several species of these insects, called
by the Arabs Jerad, but only in small quantities; and indeed it
is seldom that the northern provinces of Marocco are visited by
them in such numbers as materially to injure the vegetation.

On one occasion, however, I myself witnessed their ravages
in the neighbourhood of Tangier, and can truly say, in the
words of the Old Testament, " They covered the face of the
whole earth, so that the land was darkened, and they did eat
every herb of the land, and all the fruit of the trees which the
hail had left, and there remained not any green thing in the
trees or in the herbs of the field." *

At the period to which I refer, the locust first appeared near
Tangier in the winged form, and did not commit much injury,
but settling along the sea-coast, deposited their eggs and died.
Some months afterwards, in July, if I remember rightly, the
grub first appeared, and was about the size of what is commonly
called the lion-ant.   A price had been set by several European

* Exodus x. 15.

residents at Tangier upon each pound of eggs that was brought by the natives, and many thousand pounds' weight by this means were destroyed, but, apparently, it was of no avail; it was but the drop of water from the ocean; for soon the whole face of the country around was blackened by columns of these voracious insects; and as they marched on in their desolating track, neither the loftiest barriers, nor water, nor fire, daunted them. Quenching with their numbers the hottest fire, the rear of the dreadful columns passed over the devoted bodies of those who had preceded them. Across ditches, streams, or rivers, it was the same. On, on they marched, and as the foremost ranks of the advanced columns were drowned, their bodies formed the raft for those that followed; and where there seemed most resistance to their progress, thither did the destructive insect appear to swarm in the greatest numbers.

One European resident at Tangier, the Consul-General for Sweden, who possessed a beautiful garden in the neighbourhood, abounding with the choicest flowers and shrubs of Europe and Africa, waged for a long time successful war against them. His large garden had the advantage of a high wall, and outside this barrier he had stationed labourers, hired for the purpose of destroying the invading columns. Often did the Moslems shake their heads, and, predicting sooner or later the destruction of his garden, exclaim against the wickedness and folly of the Nazarene in attempting to avert the decrees of fate. At one time it had been hoped that this beautiful spot, a favourite resort of the Europeans, had been saved, for, whilst all around had been rendered bare and desolate, the garden yet rejoiced in a luxuriance of vegetation.

But the day soon came in which the Moslems' predictions were to be fulfilled. The locusts, ceasing to be crawling grubs, put forth their wings, and took flight. Myriads and myriads, attracted by the freshness, alighted on this oasis of the desert, and in a few hours every green blade disappeared, the very bark of the fruit-trees being gnawed in such a manner as to render them incapable of producing fruit the ensuing year.

At length, a favourable wind having arisen, the locusts took flight from around Tangier, and the sky was darkened by their countless hosts. Vast numbers of them were driven into the

sea, as shoals of their putrid bodies washed back upon the coast
proved to us. It not unfrequently happens that the stench of
the dead bodies of this insect causes very bad contagious fevers.

The female locusts, when full of eggs, become an article of
food with the Moors. They are boiled in salt water in the same
manner as shrimps, which they resemble in taste, but it requires
some resolution at first to get the monster into your mouth.
When in the grub state they are greedily devoured by the wild
boar, jackal, fox, and other wild animals, and on taking wing
they are attacked by storks, hawks, and almost all the feathered
tribe.

In the present instance, the amount of mischief which we
noticed was comparatively small, yet it was sufficient to give an
appearance of singular desolation to the space over which it
extended, and to lead my Spanish friend to expatiate upon the
subject. Having, however, concluded his entomological disqui-
sitions, the Don very graciously intimated to the story-teller
that he might resume his narrative. Off at once set the Arab,
nothing loth.

" It was at this time, O Nazarene gentleman! when such
reports were abroad, that there happened to be travelling over
the hill of Dar-el-Clow an aged Taleb * on his return from the
village of E'Mzòra † to his native place near Tangier. As the
old priest reached the ' vale of murders,' he goaded on his mule
into a hurried amble, being somewhat cheered at seeing a party
of muleteers about a mile before him, who had already gained
the summit of the hill, and whom he now anxiously strove to
join, for his memory was full of what he had heard when repos-
ing the night before with another traveller in the mosque-hut of
E'Mzòra; and the horrid tale which now depressed his spirit
shall be told you, as we travel on, that you Nazarenes may know
of what the Western Saracens are capable under the tempting
influence of gold and silver.

* A Taleb is the name given in Marocco to a public scribe or notary;
and, as religious and civil law with Mohamedans is one and the same thing,
the Taleb is priest as well as scribe.

† Close to the village of E'Mzòra is the site of an heliacal temple, where-
of, among numerous remains now prostrate, one stone, called vulgarly by
the Moors Al Ootsed, or " the peg," stands yet erect, and is of such large
dimensions that it would not discredit the stupendous structure on Salisbury
Plain.

" This was the tale to which the venerable Taleb had listened in fear and trembling :—

" Two Hebrew pedlars, who had made some little gain by selling gewgaws to the Arab women, were trudging back to Tangier, when they were assaulted in a woody spot of the Taleb's present track by an armed mountaineer. To offer resistance to a Moslem is the last thought that ever occurs to infidel Jews, so opening quickly the little bag of bontquees,* they instantly swallowed the gold.

" The robber searched them, but was disappointed of his prize ; but he soon suspected where they had hidden the gains which he well knew they had made in the neighbouring encampments. The poor Jews, trembling, protested their poverty, and kissed the feet of the highwayman, craving his mercy ; when the merciless ruffian took advantage of their position, and stabbed his suppliants to the heart, and, ripping them up, snatched his bloody booty from their entrails.

" ' Stop, or I shoot,' grated on the old man's ear as he was pondering on this fearful story. He quickly reined in his mule, and groaned out ' May God have mercy on me !' ' Your prayer is heard, O Moostafa the learned,' said the same hollow voice ; ' leave your beast and come hither.' The Taleb dismounted, his teeth chattering as he tottered towards the mysterious speaker, who now, in the sing-song tone used by the Mohamedans while reciting the Koran, began to repeat the *Fatha'*, or first chapter of the holy book.

" ' Praise be to God, the Lord of all creatures, the . most merciful, the King of the day of judgment ; thee do we worship, and of thee do we implore assistance ; direct us in the —'

" ' I never could get further,' said the unseen speaker, ' and I remember the time, venerable father, when your long stick, that now, I see, serves as your support, would have been rapped sharply over my *six fingers.*'

" ' God is great !' exclaimed the Taleb : ' What ! is it Alee the six-fingered ? O Alee ! Alee ! thou wouldst not have come to this, if God had willed you should remember his holy words.' Then raising up his staff, as the old pedagogue would have done

---

* Small gold pieces equal in value to about eight shillings each.

had he been safe within his school, he prompted the *quondam*
pupil, his ruling passion for teaching conquering all his fears.

" ' Direct us in the right way,—say that, Alee,—in the way
of those to whom thou hast been gracious, who walk uprightly,
not of those against whom thou art incensed, nor of those who
go astray.—— But where art thou, my son, or is it thy spirit
that speaketh? for I heard the Bokhàry killed thee in the month
of Doolhedja last.'

" Alee, who had been well concealed in the hollow trunk of a
large and ancient cork-tree, startled the old schoolmaster by his
sudden appearance, and, taking hold of the hem of his garment,
kissed it reverently.

" ' O my son,' said the Taleb, ' I grievously fear thy sins
will be on my head! Return with me to Bendeesham and your
friends! Still there is hope, for has not the Prophet written—
If ye turn aside from the grievous sins which ye are forbidden
to commit, we will cleanse you from your faults, and will intro-
duce you into Paradise with an honourable entry?'

" Alee, starting from his knees, exclaimed, ' Does the lion,
to whom God has given strength above all beasts, does he content himself with a sheep while the herd of oxen are within his
grasp? Why, then, should I live in misery and slavery, since
the Ruler of nature has given me the strength and activity of a
lion? Whence,' he continued, in an indignant tone which made
the old man tremble, ' whence do sultans and their soldiery—
those human falcons—derive their right of preying on the weak?
Thinkest thou that I and thousands of bearded men kissed the
dust, the other day, in the Meshwa, before him who claims the
title of Meer al Moomenin (Prince of Believers), from good
will and affection?—No! nor is it from such motive that you
and your brethren pay into his coffers your scanty gains! What
cause have I for abandoning my mode of subsisting in this world,
or for fearing punishment in the next, whilst the defender of your
faith breaks the Prophet's law by rapine and extortion, and yet
lives at ease in his conscience, so long as he has the power to
do wrong with impunity? I am not more of a freebooter than
he is; only I practise on a much smaller scale. My edict is—
Stand, or I fire! My prime minister is my good gun and an
unerring aim.

" ' Hark ! I hear the distant tread of camels ; come, old man, this night thou shalt be the guest of the Spirit of the Woods ;' and he laughed wildly. ' Mount your mule, and I will lead the way.'

" The old man, fearing to refuse, followed the outlaw. They scrambled their way through thickest copses, trespassing on the very lair of the lynx, the jackal, and the boar, who, roused, retreated grumbling, after their fashion, at such strange intrusion.

" The Taleb thought that the way they went looked like one where human feet had never trod before, and so it was most probably, for Alee had avoided detection by never travelling twice over the same path.

" The old schoolmaster began to feel himself very uneasy as, muttering the word Allah ! Allah ! a hundred times, he followed his extraordinary conductor, grievously fearing that but little good would come to himself or his mule. At length they reached a jungle of briers, apparently impassable ; and Taleb Moostafa said, with a trembling voice, ' It seems to me, my son, that you have missed the track.'

" Alee made no answer, but having first bent down, as if to examine the ground, uttered a sound like the bleating of a kid, which was soon answered by a shrill whistle, that made the old man's heart sink within him, and put a bridle on his tongue.

" ' All is right,' said Alee, going to a spot where the jungle seemed the thickest; then listening a while, he threw back a wicket of the living brier, made in such a manner as not to be detected even by a hunter's observing eye. This they passed through, and then the briers were cautiously replaced. Winding along a narrow path cut through the thicket, they came upon an open space, through which ran a clear stream. On its bank the outlaw had formed a hut, but so thatched as to be with difficulty distinguished from the surrounding thicket foliage.

" As they entered, a young woman in a loose dress ran forward to meet and embrace the outlaw.

" ' Well, Rahmana, I have not been able to keep my promise to bring the bracelets and handkerchiefs; for just as the kafla was coming up, our venerable uncle here made his appearance on the highway, and I could not let my good old schoolmaster

F

pass our dwelling without a welcome; so, my dear Rahmana,
you must make ready some savoury dish out of the flesh of the
wild cow * I shot yesterday; for I think our guest must be very
hungry. As he spoke he turned round to the old man, who had
sat down with his back turned to the fair partner of his wild
pupil.

"'Come, Seedy Moostafa,' said Alee, 'the Spirit of the Woods
is not jealous of his Houri. Why is woman made lovely, but to
be looked upon? and what were our eyes given us for by the All-
wise, but to behold beautiful things? Rahmana, go, ask the
Taleb's blessing, and then prepare the kesksoo.'

"To hear was to obey with old Moostafa upon the present
occasion; so raising the hood of his white geelab, he looked upon
Rahmana; who bent to kiss his hand, and having received a
blessing, left him in order to prepare the meal.

"'This damsel is truly beautiful—blessed be God!—and seems
happy with you in this wild scene: may I ask you, my son, how
came she here?'

"Alee took out a small cane carved in Arabic; then jerking
out on the hollow between his thumb and forefinger a long snuff
of Tetuan tobacco, offered it to the Taleb: and looking at him,
steadfastly replied: 'For my wife I paid no dowry; yet I hold
her dearer, ay, dearer, I dare say, than the Kaid of Alcassar can
prize either of his four, though for one of them alone he gave a
dower of a thousand *Mitzakel*. Now, hear how I brought my
fair one to her bridegroom's home.

"'Having one morning taken up my position on a high rock
that gave a wide command of view, I remained perched, like the
eagle, watching for my prey; when a party of travellers appeared
slowly winding up the hill. The principal persons were preceded
by their baggage-animals with their drivers; behind these rode on
an ambling mule a venerable man, whose dress bespoke some
wealthy Fas merchant; and by his side, on a stout pony, rode,
after the fashion of a man, a female closely muffled up.

"'I descended cautiously from the height; then taking my

* Within a very few years wild cattle abounded in the woods of Boomar;
they were of a dun colour, had very long horns, and were of lighter frame
than the tame cattle. When wounded they were very dangerous. The last
of these wild animals was, I understand, killed about four years ago.

stand by a fountain near the highway, waited with a cocked gun the travellers' approach.

" 'I had already taken sure aim at one of the muleteers, who having a brace of pistols slung over his geelab, might, I thought, prove my most troublesome opponent.

" ' As the party reached the fountain, the old man dismounted from his mule, then helped his female companion to alight, whose beauty, which you have so deservedly admired, I then first beheld; for as she dismounted, her haik caught in the stirrup, which drew it from her grasp, and unveiled the hallowed features. From that moment I resolved she should be mine, and, God willing, without bloodshed.

" ' The old man having seated her at the verge of the wood, in the shade, ordered the muleteers to push on with the baggage-animals towards Tangier, and said that he would rejoin them with his daughter as soon as he had performed his ablution and pro-stration; for the shortened shadow told it was about mid-day, and the hour of prayer. I now felt convinced my prize would be easily won, for the protector of the fair was too infirm to offer resistance, yet still I waited my best opportunity.

" ' The old man, having performed sundry ablutions at the fountain, took from his saddle-bags a fine Fas rug, on which, having spread it east and west, he began his adoration; but find-ing, I suppose, the surface of the ground in that spot too rough for his aged limbs, he moved to a level plot of turf some fifty yards down the hill, and there in perfect comfort recommenced his genuflections.'

" ' God forbid,' said old Moostafa, ' that at such a moment thou shouldst have wronged him.'

" ' It was God's will,' continued the robber : ' but listen.

" ' Leaving my gun against a tree, I crept cautiously through the thicket, until I reached its border, where sat Rahmana closely wrapped in her haik. I was about to carry my purpose into execution, when the clatter of horses' hoofs was heard fast ascend-ing the hill, and obliged me again to retreat into the bushes. The new comers proved to be a body of cavalry escorting prisoners, whose hands and feet were strongly bound in chains. The party halted at the fountain for a little time to refresh their horses; and then moved quickly on again. The old man was yet at prayers, though I could perceive he was about to conclude them. Scarcely were the horsemen out of sight, when I crept again with noiseless step towards the damsel. Her back was turned: I took off my slippers, and crawling upon hands and feet, cautiously approached close to her: then giving a glance at the old man, whose forehead was pressed to the ground, I pounced on my prey, and pressing the haik over her mouth, I lifted her in my arms, and dashed into the forest, regaining my gun as I passed the tree.

" ' The poor girl was sadly frightened, and endeavoured to give the alarm to her aged parent; but he could not have heard her stifled screams. I brought her to this hut, and loosening the veil, gazed on her features. A death-like paleness had come over them, and her eyes were closed. I shuddered as I thought that Azrael, the arch-robber of mankind, had snatched her from me. A gentle heaving of the bosom told me, however, that her fate was not yet written. She looked so pale and sorrow-stricken, that for a moment I almost resolved to restore her to her father; but then, I reflected that a worse lot might befall her than to be the wife of one who already loved her so fervently as I did; for perhaps, reasoned I, she is destined to become one of a numerous harem of some old dolt in Tangier;—and this,' said the Arab, interrupting himself, ' was just the case.

" ' I bathed,' continued Alee, ' her forehead with cool water from this clear stream: she opened her eyes, but shrunk back on beholding me, and cried out, "O father, save me;" and then again she closed her long eyelashes, studded with liquid diamonds. Long, long, it was that she remained disconsolate. She would take no food all the day and night, and I watched her almost insensible form. On the morning I again endeavoured to soothe her, but the only words she uttered were, " Where is my father?" I swore to her by my beard that he was unharmed, at the same time declaring my passion for her, and that I was her slave. Still she rejected food. I continued to watch her with the tenderest care, and vowed never to sleep or eat till she became assured I meant her no harm.

" ' At length hunger obliged her to taste something; and then, poor girl, after many days, she took courage to converse with me. She told me who she was, and that her father, in spite of all her entreaties, had resolved to have married her to the old administrator of customs in Tangier, a husband aged enough to remember the first plague.—But now,' said the robber, ' we are husband and wife, and only wish for your blessing and a written contract to be as happy a pair as the doves, *God's proclaimers,* * that are wooing over our heads.'

" ' That shall be granted,' said the old Taleb ; ' but, my good Alee, what became of her father ?'

" ' Why,' said Alee, ' I little know ; though, in truth, I heard one of a party of travellers, while sitting under the tree, the very tree from which I carried off Rahmana, relate that a beautiful girl of Fas had been carried off from her father, and that the old man was persuaded it was the *Jin* of the Woods ; for although at prayers within a few paces of her, he had seen nothing, and had heard nothing.'

" The next morning before break of day Alee conducted his guest through the forest to the high road, and on taking leave presented him with thirty mitzakel, and cloth of the finest texture sufficient to make a soolliam, which would have done honour to a kady. But, O noble Christian, the old man, as I shall now relate, was little worthy the confidence and bounty of his former pupil.

" Not many days succeeding this strange adventure of Taleb Moostafa with the Spirit of the Woods, a message was dispatched by the Kaid of Tangier to the court, which was then in Marocco, giving full particulars of the abode and person of the secret evil-doer, declaring that he who had carried off the merchant's daughter was no other than the six-fingered Alee. On that very day a considerable number of horsemen were ordered to scour the wood of Dar A'clon ;† but they did so without success. They had penetrated even to the very cave where the scene took place which I have just described, where the yet smouldering embers and other recent vestiges showed that the strange inhabitant had received as true information of their intention as they of his abode.

" Daring robberies were now committed day after day in the Forest of Maucora, about three days' journey from Alee's late

* An epithet given to the dove by the Moors, from the motion they make when cooing being similar to that of the prostrations of a Moslem at prayer

† Meaning the House of "Clon," a famous robber in former days. The house no longer exists, but there is to be seen at the top of the hill a cave, whither robbers yet resort occasionally.

retreat. A party of Arabs had laid in wait for Alee, and succeeded in wounding him ; but, as usual, Alee escaped, sending three of their number to rejoice the hearts of the Houris in Paradise.

·" A proclamation was issued by the sultan, and sent to all governors of provinces and towns, to all kaids and sheikhs of this western empire, ordering them to use all diligence to take alive or to kill Alee the six-fingered, the plague and torment of the universe. All were obedient to the Shereefian edict, yet still the outlaw kept the country in alarm.´ Wealthy travellers and rich-laden kaflas took redoubled precaution against the formidable Alee, whose rapid movements made many people believe that he had a charmed life, and could be in ten places at one time.

" Alee, however, wisely kept friends with the country folk, and the poor especially, often enriching them at rich men's cost : it was indeed strongly suspected that the people of many camps and hamlets had connived with him ; nay, that they even were associated with him in more than one of his forays."

CHAPTER VII.

Story of Robber continued—The Sheikh's Mare—The Message—the Reward
—Alee keeps his word—The Dog's Bribe—Description of the Mare—
Shot at a Pigeon, but killed a Crow—War not against the Devil—The
Siege—The Ambuscade—Roast Pork—The Failure—The Flight.

"WHILST the sultan was contriving Alee's destruction, the
robber's famous horse, on which he had often escaped from justice, died from over-exertion, after saving his master's life while
hotly pursued by a troop of cavalry. Now there was an Arab
sheikh who governed a camp in the neighbourhood of Alcassar,
and who, amongst much rare and precious property, possessed a
mare of marvellous powers. Her swiftness was that of the east
wind, and by the most true God, I swear, she was a thorough-
bred deafener.* Her dam, it was said, had surpassed in beauty
and speed all the horses in the world. Her sire, it was firmly
believed, was the famous stallion of the sea, called Moha al
Bahr.† No sooner did Alee—now without a horse—hear of the
famous mare, than he coveted this most precious of the rich
sheikh's goods, and vowed that he would have her by fair means
or by foul.

" It happened that, in one of his marauding expeditions, a
follower of this very sheikh fell into the hands of Alee. A free
passage was promised to this man, on condition of his carrying
faithfully a message to his master, touching the mare. This
message was couched in extremely polite, but rather decisive
terms ; to the effect that, at an appointed time and place, he, the
sheikh, would be pleased to send the mare ; adding that this was
suggested to save both the sheikh and himself much trouble, and,
it might be, some bloodshed ; for, were not the mare sent as
directed. he should forthwith take her by force, and no power,

* The Moors' epithet for a horse that deafens the rider by the speed with
which it rushes through the air.

† There is a Moorish legend telling of such an animal on the coast of
Arabia, where it is supposed the finest Arabs are bred.

if so it pleased God, should hinder him. He then dismissed the man unharmed, but with a dreadful threat of vengeance, if he did not fulfil his mission faithfully.

" The poor envoy soon found cause to rue his having undertaken this office; for on presenting himself to the sheikh, and delivering Alee's message, he was ordered to receive instantly one hundred stripes of the dreadful filaly* for his barefaced impudence. This was all the attention shown to the robber's demand and threat. Well indeed might the haughty sheikh regard it lightly, for this mare of all mares was picketed every night in front of his own tent, and in the centre of the dooar, around which prowled packs of hungry dogs, watchful as the moon, and who, with little provocation, would make a meal of any stranger who trespassed on their domain after dusk.

" It was on a dreary day in the month of January, while fierce wind and torrents of rain raged from the heavens, that a man in the dress of a courier, his hooded geelab tucked up and girded round his loins, his feet clothed in a pair of stout sandals, a small dagger stuck in his girdle, and a palmetto basket slung over his shoulder for a budget, was seen making hasty way on the high road to Alcassar Kibeer, and not till between the *Mood Aloolee* and the *Sebbah* † did he deviate from the main track and take the direction of a camp of the *Oolad Ensair*,‡ thence some half-hour's distance. The gloomy eve turned to a black night, while a sea of the heaviest rain fell pelting from above.

" The disguised courier, for it was none other than Alee himself, halted as he neared the camp, and finding all quiet, except now and then the howl of a dog, he planned his approach; and now on hands and feet advanced cautiously towards the pen where the sheep were kept, in the eye of the wind, for fear the hungry hounds should sniff him. Snatching a ' father of wool '§ out of the pen, he squeezed him in his grasp, and retraced his steps some fifty yards; then drawing his dagger, sacrificed the mutton in the name of God, and making a prayer for his success, proceeded to cut up the carcass into some fifty bits.

" Taking these in the skirts of his geelab, he moved on some

* The usual Moorish scourge, so called as being made of strips of Tafilelt leather.
† Between two and five o'clock in the morning.
‡ The sons of eagles.   § *Abou Souf,* or a sheep.

few yards and listened: all was quiet. Then he imitated the barking cry of a jackal; and the well-known sound was re-sponded to by several of the village pack. He repeated it, and two or three fierce hounds rushed towards him. He threw them a bone: growling and fighting ensued, which soon attracted the whole pack of ill-fed dogs. Delicious morsels—sufficient to bribe and to satisfy the hungry maws of all comers—were thrown to them: and henceforward the enemy required no watchword with which to enter the unguarded camp. So, taking a bridle he had stowed away in his basket for the purpose, and grasping his dagger, he walked boldly to the sheikh's abode of felicity.

"There stood the prize—black as the night, but her eye gleamed like a star! There she stood inviting her ravisher. Her figure was like"—(and the narrator paused, as if at a loss for a comparison)—"picture to yourself, O Nazarene, an animal yet more beautiful, more lively, than my steed, and you have it. She snorted and reared, but Alee was quicker than the heels of a thorough-bred, for planting his vice-like hand on her nostrils, he donned the bridle, cut the pickets, and now vaulted on her back.

"'Most generous sheikh,' cried the 'six-fingered.' Nobody answered, 'O possessor of fine horses! O Sheikh Hamon!'

"'What's the matter, and who is there?' said a gruff voice from within the tent.

"'God give you a prosperous morning, Sheikh Hamon,' said Alee: 'I have kept my word and come for the mare; may the All-bountiful send you a better.' No sooner said he these words, than he darted off full gallop into darkness.

"Sheikh Hamon, with cocked gun, rushed to the rescue, and caught a glimpse of a black figure making off at full speed. 'Devils and demons,' cried he in despair, 'she shall die rather than be another man's.' He fired, and down fell his object. A wild laugh echoed at a distance. The sheikh rushed towards the fallen object: all the villagers were up in arms—'Seize him, Mohamed—Bind him, Salem—Bring him dead or alive, Mus-tafa,' cried the frantic sheikh: 'if I have killed my —— (and he could not for grief utter the name of his mare) my loss is irretrievable; but I have done a service to the sultan and the world.'

"The forms of half-naked Arabs, with torches, guns, and

daggers, gleamed all around, and now they rushed towards the fallen mass, and a shout of surprise and yet of gladness was given as they discovered that the angry passion of their chief had been vented on one of his finest black bulls, the plague of the village, for many persons had been gored of late; and as they were ignorant of Alee's apparition, they all supposed it had met with its well-deserved fate for having attacked their chief when returning from his matins. They dragged the carcass before the sheikh's tent, who, on beholding his victim, plucked his beard in fury, then hung his head, and with solemn voice exclaimed—'War not against the devil—God's will be done,' and returned into his tent.

"The loss of the mare, and the extraordinary conduct of the sheikh, were not known in the village until next day.—Alee rode that mare till the day of his death.

" 'Though he possess the charm of Abd-Errachman, the Soosy—though he be in league with the dark One himself—this day shall he render account to Him who is the Almighty Judge of crime!' Thus spoke a doughty kaid, who, armed to the teeth, and mounted on a prancing horse, was accompanied by some fifty followers, all in warlike trim.

" 'Look,' said the kaid to his kleefa (lieutenant), as they reached a dark and lonely ravine in the wood of Boamar—'look at these gouts of blood, which—still as crimson as on the day poor Sheikh Selim, the bearded, was here villainously murdered —call for the vengeance of all who would fight in the path of righteousness. Here let us then arrange our plans, and swear not to abandon our task till we have fulfilled the mandates of our lord the sultan; and let every man take the precaution of adding a silver okeea * to the ball, for thus alone can be broken the charm of the malicious one.'

" 'The Fatha†—let the Fatha be said,' they all with one voice exclaimed; and Taleb Abd-el-Kader, a military moolah,‡ with hands uplifted, gabbled over the sacred words:

" 'Praise be to God, the Lord of all creatures, the most merciful, the King of the day of judgment. Thee do we worship,

* A piece of money worth about 3d. sterling.
† 1st chapter of the Koran, used as a prayer.
‡ Priest.

and of thee do we implore assistance. Direct us in the right way; in the way of those to whom thou hast been gracious, who walk uprightly: not of those against whom thou art incensed, nor of those who go astray.'

" The stronghold of the besieged freebooter was a wood, about two miles long, by half a mile in breadth; impenetrable in many parts from the thick briers and close-set bushes. To attempt to beard the robber in his den was considered too hazardous a deed: it was therefore determined tò set fire to the wood, in the quarter whence the wind was blowing, and to lay wait for the fugitive on the opposite side. Thus they felt assured that, between fire and sword, they were certain to destroy him. Kaid Mohktar now proceeded to station his men, in companies of six, at all the outlets of the wood; then taking with him a few chosen men, he rode round to the opposite side to commence the work of destruction.

" Some dried leaves and branches having been collected, a light was struck, and the conflagration commenced. At first a small column of smoke curled up in the air: it was soon followed by a volume of flame towering to the height of the tallest trees, and withering with its great heat every green bush, ere it reduced it to dust and charcoal. The fire strided on: and what was lately an impenetrable thicket became a waste of smoking ashes.

" The kaid, with his attendants, continued busy firing the wood, wherever the wind would favour the progress of the flame. Success seemed to attend the stratagem; and all were waiting, though not without fear, to discover which outlet the terrible, and until now unvanquished, Alee would choose for his sally.

" Then it was that a flame rose suddenly from the very centre of the wood, at a spot some three hundred yards distant from the advancing fire. It blazed, it crackled, and rolled on with a headlong vigour of destruction; and at intervals was heard the rending crash of some giant tree, that had for ages braved all the other elements, but now lowered its noble head.

" ' Who,' cried the Kaid in wild despair, ' who but this accursed fiend would have thought of such a scheme? See! he has fired the wood in the centre, and when all around shall be burnt, he will choose his point of escape.'

" To prevent this, the Kaid had now to change his plan; and

posted his men all round the wood in parties of three. They had commenced their attack early in the morning; it was now about noon. The fire they had first kindled had just reached the yet smoking embers of the conflagration in the centre, and that, in its turn, had carried its ravages to the opposite border. One small path still remained green; all around was a mass of flame and smoke. The Kaid had stationed himself in a watercourse with three men. Birds and animals were flying with terror all around, heedless of man's presence; and ever and anon a frantic boar would gallop down the watercourse.

" ' Allah!' said one of the party, as an 'abou snau'* passed with bristles half singed from his back, and smoking from the fire; 'if he tastes as well as he smells, I could make up my mind to sell myself to the devil and dine on his carcass. God forgive me for saying so!'

" 'Hush!' said the Kaid in a low voice; 'he comes; and, O merciful God, he comes our way! Be steady and resolute.'

" A mounted figure could now be seen moving rapidly over the burning embers. His pace increased as he neared the ambuscade; and the slight figure of a female, her garments blackened with the fire and smoke, and her long hair streaming in the breeze, was clinging to the waist of the robber. Mounted on a jet-black steed, that, with blood-red extended nostril and foaming mouth, bounded as a deer over the huge rocks, Alee, with levelled gun, dashed straight towards the party. The Kaid had now made sure aim, and, raising a shout to bring together the line of valiants posted along the wood, was about to pull the trigger, when a deadly shot brought him a corpse to the ground. His three attendants stood firm, waiting with levelled guns their adversary's nearer approach, to give him a warm reception, and avenge the death of their chief.

" Alee in an instant had given the gun to Rahmana, and, drawing his sword, now flew like lightning on his opponents. The black mare, as if she knew her owner's danger, redoubled her speed; and in an instant the robber was on them, and received their fire unhurt. Man after man rolled on the ground: all fell who came within his reach, whilst he eluded every blow of his enemies.

* *Abou Snau,* ' father of tusks.'

"The whole body of troops had now approached. The balls flew thickly; but, still unharmed, the hero and his well-beloved pursued their course. Nay, some declared that the balls were heard to rebound from his body back upon his assailants; and it must have been so, for there was a second man of the party killed by a shot-wound besides the kaid—upon whose soul be mercy!

"Alee having distanced his pursuers, slackened his pace; he sheathed his sword, and reloaded his gun. One horseman yet pursued him boldly. Alee descended a steep ravine, and, turning close round the side of the opposite hill, reined in the mare. The well-mounted pursuer was not many yards in his rear. Alee waited him, and soon, with drawn sword and shouts of vengeance, he turned the corner.

"'Fire!' cried Rahmana, 'or we are lost!'

"'Let him come,' said her husband; and as the enemy approached, Alee recognised in him one of the Bokhàry blacks who had vowed vengeance on him the day of his feat at Marocco in presence of the sultan.

"'Join the Blow-giver!' shouted Alee, as he shot him through the brains.

"'And now,' said he to his wife, 'jump up into my saddle, while I mount yon horse of the swarthy black, which seems to be a good one. Hark! tne troops are again in pursuit of us. On—on! for we must ride till the morrow dawns on us in the wood of Sahel.'

"Next morning the fugitive and his wife were safe in their little tent of camel's hair in the Sahel, unmolested and undiscovered; and the body of cavalry returned, brow-beaten, to Tangier, to tell a dreadful tale of wonders.

"Alee, with a keen eye, scrutinized the path and bushes; and, following the fibre of aloe with which he had encircled their abode, found it unbroken except in the path they had entered. His stock of food, which he had left there since his last visit, was also safe."

CHAPTER VIII.

Continuation of Journey—The Hyæna—Alarby the Silent—The Race—
  Moorish justice—The *Jins*—The Wig—The Magician—The owner of the
  " rat-tailed " resumes his story—The marriage of Jilaly—The Offering—
  Alee is seized—His Escape—The Pursuit—A sad Scene—The Burial—
  Interruption of our Story—Alee a Mourner—Sanctuary violated—Im-
  prisonment— Sentence — Torture — Death and Burial — Executions in
  Marocco.

AT no part of our journey had the scenery been more pleasing
than at that where we now arrived. It was the entrance of the
wood of Sahel, formed of cork-tree, oak, wild-pear, and locust-
tree, with underwood of furze, tamarisk, and myrtle. Protected
by the thick foliage from the scorching rays of the sun, we
travelled on pleasantly for several hours. The Mallem had
taken the lead, and now conducted us through the thicket by a
narrow path, which our loaded animals had some difficulty in
threading. It was marked with tracks of wild animals, among
which I was told those of the hyæna, and sometimes of the pan-
ther, might be recognised by the huntsman's eye.

I have often been amused by the difference of tone in which
the Arab sportsmen express themselves when speaking of the
different animals of chace. When they talk of the lion, it is
always as if they considered him a particularly gentlemanly personage ; and they treat panthers and boars civilly enough. But
their contempt of the cowardice and stupidity of the hyæna has
no limit ; indeed its Arabic name, " dbaa," means addle-headed
or stupid.

On the present occasion the Hadj was very severe upon them.

" The dull-witted knaves," he said, " fancy that if they can
hide their head in a hole, all the rest of their body will be invi-
sible ; and be assured, O Nazarene ! that the Arab huntsmen
are not slow to take advantage of their folly. I remember,"
continued the Hadj, " accompanying a friend of mine to a
cavern which he had marked down as the abode of one of these

rapscalions. We took with us no other weapons than our daggers and a long rope. Having reached the mouth of the cavern, which was situated in a thicket, my companion, stooping down, peered within; and could perceive the hyæna nestled in a corner, with its head thrust into a cavity of the rock. Turning to me, he said—and he took care to speak loud enough for the beast to hear him—'Did you say that the hyæna was here? You must be mistaken, for he is not here now. O no! they call him a stupid fellow; but he is no fool: if he was, he would be here.' Then, entering the mouth of the cavern with his eye upon the beast, my companion continued: 'O what folly to suppose the hyæna would be here! It is quite light; I can see everything; but the dbaa, poor fellow, he is gone. O no, he is not such a fool as we call him!' Then, cautiously approaching the animal, with his dagger in one hand and the rope in the other, talking loud all the time, 'Yes, yes,' he said, 'it would be very different with me if the hyæna was here. He is a brave fellow; he is not afraid of two men,—no, nor of a dozen. He is a clever fellow, though men do abuse him.' Then suddenly he slipped a noose of the rope round his hind-legs, and shouted to me, 'Pull away! pull away! He is here, the rascal, the coward, the fool! Pull, pull away!' So the hyæna was drawn out of the cave, and we dispatched him with our daggers."

The Hadj said, that even when the hyæna is ensconced in a hole with his head towards the huntsmen, they frequently thrust a bone towards him, which the stupid beast will seize hold of with his teeth; and the huntsmen, taking advantage of his gripe, drag him out, and then dispatch him by the blow of a club, or with a stone.

During the time the Hadj was giving us this anecdote, we had become more entangled in the thicket. Every now and then, my knees encountering the thorny furze, or when closely embraced by a fond bramble, I grumbled angry words against the Mallem for having left the beaten track; on which our hardy guide, to my further discomfort, quickened his pace, promising that we should soon arrive at a large village, and resume the wider and more easy road. After another half-hour's scrambling we came suddenly upon the promised village, which was situated in a fine valley abounding with many a cool and refreshing spring.

"Here lives," said the Hadj, "*Old Alarby Sooktsee* (Alarby the Silent), from whom, you must remember, son of the English, you purchased your favourite horse."

"Never shall I forget old Alarby," I replied; "but we have not time to stop, or I would send for the old breeder of horses. Often has he begged that I would give back his child, as he calls my favourite Arab."

This Alarby was a curious fellow, enthusiastic in his attachment to horses; and so redundantly eloquent in their praise, that why he was denominated "the silent" was always a mystery to me.

On going into our stables a month or two ago with a friend, a young Frenchman, to show him my pet, we found the old fellow kissing *Arab's* forehead with great affection. The sagacious animal pricked up his ears, and evidently recognised his former master.

"God be blessed!" said Alarby; "he remembers me—the darling! And I could tell my own horse among a thousand: I knew him by his silken coat, his graceful form, his beautiful little head."

And the old fellow's eyes glistened, and he chuckled, as he said, "I knew him! I knew him!"

My friend was not a little amused at this burst of tenderness in a horse-dealer; and drew him out, nothing loath, into a long rhodomontade history of myself and my horse, or rather of my horse and myself; which, as characteristic of Arab feeling, I will give as nearly as I can in the very words he used.

"Hear, O Christian!" said old Alarby the Silent, and, though safe from all eaves-dropping, he spoke at first in a whisper; but, by degrees, as his energy increased, he became loud and vehement,—"hear the feats of my horse, and how, when mounted upon him, the son of the English encountered the Arab tribes:—It was when the Fekee Abd Eslam Eslowy first came to Tangier that there was born to him a son by his favourite slave; and the tribes of Ib-dowa and Tleg-el-Kholot, mustering some thousand horsemen, came down to this city, protected of the Lord, to congratulate Seedy—our master—upon the event, and present their offerings.   On the eve of their arrival the two tribes assembled upon the sea-shore, to indulge in *Lab-el-barode;* and O, such chargers! such gazelles!   Praised be God for his bounty to men, as it was displayed by those matchless horses upon that happy day!   The hills were crowded with the men of Tangier, and of all the country round; and from every crack in the old town-wall peered the lovely wives of the Faithful, through their muffled haiks, encouraging the hearts of all around by their shrill yells of joy.

"And now the men of Ib-dowy charged in bodies of two and three score; and Salem the Swarthy would be seen in the race standing on his head; then followed the Tleeg and Kholot. And, as they galloped, each horseman, standing in his saddle, would shift steeds with his neighbour, discharging their guns as they reached the goal.   It was a sight to have rejoiced even the dwellers in Paradise!

"Well, Christian, be it known to you that during the sport I observed a Frank join the spectators.   He was mounted on an iron-grey, and his horse, moving with arched crest and uplifted tail, seemed barely to touch the ground.   I looked again, and I said within my heart, 'That horse is my breeding, or no man's!' In another moment I knew him to be mine; for I recognised the purchaser of my horse, the son of the English, as he turned his head towards me.

"Many were the taunts the Christian received from the Arabs as they passed on returning from the charge.   They laughed at his saddle and bridle, and called upon him to join in their charges, if he dared.   This he refused, saying he had no gun, and that he preferred being a spectator.

"Now I drew nigh to where he had taken his stand, and I overheard one of the Tleeg, who had reined in his beautiful black charger, in order to scrutinize more closely the young Christian's accoutrements, say, 'Is not this the haughty Nazarene, who, as he passed by our tents last spring, boasted that he possessed a horse that no horse had ever beaten in the course? And now, like a true infidel, he has not the courage to acknowl-l dge his false words, or to put his sorry jade to the trial.'

"To this he who now stands by your side replied, 'An Englishman never eats his words.   I still back my horse against the

G

field; but let a proper time be chosen. If I were now to show your tribe the heels of my horse, I know that I should be insulted. Name another day, or at a later hour on this, when the multitude have left the shore, and you shall witness whether the Nazarene, with his Frank saddle and bridle, cannot put his steed into the charge.'

" 'Your hand,' said the Tleeg; ' the challenge is accepted.'

" Towards the close of the evening, when the cavalry and the spectators also were moving off, the owner of the black made a sign to the Christian, who was soon at his side. Some of those who yet remained saw this; and soon the rumour spread, even to those who had left the ground, that a Frank was about to race with a Tleeg.

" The whole body of cavalry now moved back together, and with them thousands of spectators. In the meantime the son of the English rode up to the starting-point; and I saw the Sheikh of the Tleeg dispatch five other picked horsemen to join in the race. I could perceive at the distance that my own horse, my darling little one, was placed in the middle. I trembled all over with anxiety. I, a Moslem, wished the Christian to be victorious; but how could it be otherwise, when the child of my bosom was with him?

" The distance was some six hundred paces. Off the racers started; and for the first hundred yards all were neck and neck. The people shouted, and then followed a dead silence. My darling had shot in front, and so had the black. Another shout was raised—the black was in front of all! I bit my lips, and, hiding my face, cursed within myself the Nazarene for his bad horsemanship. But the shouting ceased; I looked up again: the iron-grey was foremost! I shouted aloud, and soon the frowns of all around were upon me. O, how I wished to cry out, That horse is my breeding! But I dared not for my life.

" My child won the race, and an angry murmur ran through the crowd. But the Sheikh believed that the black had won, and, riding up to the Christian, said tauntingly, ' Who gained the race, O rebeller against God?'

" ' Saw you not, O Sheikh of fine horses,' replied your friend, ' that I was left behind? and see you not that my front is covered with sand?'

" The owner of the black horse, boiling with rage at having lost the race, while a stream of blood trickled from the sides of his charger, now interfered: ' This Nazarene,' he said, ' has beat us in nothing but his arrogance; and may God burn the grandfather of the man who sold him the horse he rides !'

" Turning to the Tleeg, the Christian said, ' Did I not warn you and all your brethren who had ridiculed me, that I should throw dust in your faces? God has willed that my horse should gain : why this ill-blood? I cannot be called arrogant; on the contrary, my countrymen might more justly accuse me of having degraded myself in joining thus with a soldier-rabble.'

" ' Silence !' said the Sheikh; ' know you not that it is an honour for a Christian to compete with the basest Mahomedan? Do you think yourself, O infidel, on a par with any one of these ?'

" ' If I disbelieved in God,' replied the Nazarene, ' I might own your superiority; but, as a Christian and an Englishman, I yield to no man.'

" ' What !' cried the Sheikh, and a dark scowl came over his face, as he brought his horse close upon his; ' darest thou, O rebellious one, hold such language? Perhaps thou pretendest to be *my* equal ?'

" ' In truth,' replied the young Christian, ' I do; and, as an Englishman, I am your superior.'

" Putting his hand to the hilt of his sword, the Sheikh dared him to repeat it.

" ' I care not for your threats,' he answered; ' and I will repeat every word that I have said.'

" The Sheikh's sword was out in an instant, and waved over the Christian's head; and several of the Tleeg discharged their guns at him, singeing his garments; and had it not been that my horse lashed with his heels at all around, and that a party of Reefians rushed among the cavalry to his rescue, the Tleeg would have been revenged.

" The blessing of the Prophet on the iron-grey, the lovely one ! and a blessing upon all his ancestors !" exclaimed old Alarby the Silent, as a wind-up to his story, which, barring a little exaggeration, was a tolerably correct account of a scrape I had got into, which, if it had not been for the opportune inter-

ference of my friends among the hunters, might have ended
rather unpleasantly. But a good many of my old companions
in the chace were on the ground; and, although I was a Christian, they gallantly stood forward to defend me.

The affair will not soon be forgotten among the Tleeg; for
when I complained of the insult to the Basha, he took up the
business in a much more serious manner than I expected. He
asked me what reparation I required. I replied, that as I felt
that the fault was partly mine, for having exposed myself
amongst the wild troops, all I demanded was an apology from
the Sheikh, to be made to me in the presence of all the tribe.

" ' That," said the Basha, " would indeed be letting these
outlaws off too easily. Shall I burn their habitations? Some
severe example must be made, or you Christians will be no
longer safe."

I besought the Fekee not to proceed to such extremities.

" Well," said he, " at your request I will be lenient."

Then, turning to his Kleefa, he said, " Let the Sheikh and a
dozen of his followers be put in prison, and not be freed until a
fine of two hundred mitzakel be paid. Let the Sheikh's flocks
and cattle be driven into Laraiche; and let it be made known to
the tribe that such is the punishment of the lawless."

In vain I petitioned against such severity; the commands
were forthwith obeyed. I suspect that the Basha had long
wished to squeeze the wealthy tribe of Tleeg, and rejoiced at the
occasion.—But to return to our journey.

A camel led through a country town in England could not
have excited more curiosity and astonishment than the appearance of my Spanish friend and myself in the wild village through
which we were passing. At each door stood whole families
gaping with amazement; whilst the younger children shrunk in
terror at beholding such strange apparitions. One youth, bolder
than the rest, having approached our party, demanded of the
Hadj what kind of beings we were. The Hadj, with a grave
face, replied that we were *Jins*, or evil spirits, which he had
caught and was conducting to Laraiche, to be shipped for the
land of the Nazarene. Upon which the lad fled howling to his
hut.

I remember poor Davidson mentioning to me the general belief he had found prevalent amongst the Arabs in those parts of the Levant which travellers seldom frequent, that the Frank is in league with devils, witches, and unearthly beings. He told me that, on more than one occasion, he had profited by such fancies, when his life had been in danger from the wild tribes among whom he had ventured. Davidson was bald, and wore at that time a toupet. A body of Arabs, having surrounded him, had commenced plundering his effects, and threatened even his life; when suddenly Davidson, calling upon them to beware how they provoked the Christian's power, dashed his false hair to the ground, saying, " Behold my locks; your beards shall go next !" The Arabs fled, abandoning their plunder.

On another occasion, when making some astronomical observations, he was so inconveniently pressed upon by a crowd of insolent Arabs, that he found it impossible to continue his operations; so, turning to them, he said, " O fools, seek ye destruction ? Know the power of the Nazarene !" Then, beckoning one of the elders to approach, he told him to look through the sextant, whilst he, slowly moving the index, informed the barbarian that he would behold the sun to leave its course and approach the earth. The Arab, pale with fright, after a momentary glance, threw himself on the ground and begged for mercy, beseeching Davidson that he would forthwith leave their land, and take compassion upon their herds and crops, upon which he felt convinced that the Nazarene had the power to inflict murrain and blight.

" We must soon part, my friend," said I, turning to the rider of the rat-tailed : " I pray thee continue thy story, and let us hear what next befell your hero, the Six-fingered."

" O Christian," said he, " I have little more to say. It was in this wood we left Alee when I broke off my story—here, on this very track, it was that the traveller, when hastening on his journey, was often startled by the well-known summons of ' Stop, or I fire !'

" Alee, as I told you, never molested the poor. Wealthy caravans or pursy traders were the sufferers; but his robberies were bloodless, unless he met with resistance or disobedience. He was, indeed, on such good terms with the villagers in whose neighbourhood he carried on his depredations, that he is said to have been daily provided with an abundance of mòna, to which each village contributed a portion; and in return, when there happened to be a marriage-feast, Alee would sometimes appear, and, bringing a gift for the bridegroom, would assist at the rejoicings.

" Now Sheikh Biteewy, of the village of ———, had made known, by the public crier, that his eldest son, Jilaly, was to take unto him for wife Fatma, the daughter of Kaid Etsiftsy.

" These were joyful news for the Six-fingered, who loved a carousal, and was fond to excess of *somets*.* So, having laid in the necessary store of provision for his wife, he promised to return to her after three days; for Rahmana was expecting soon to become a mother.

" Alee then selected from the spoils of a wealthy Israelite, who had lately fallen into his clutches, a handsome piece of brocade and a pair of massive gold anklets; and having wrapped them up in a fine silk handkerchief, of Fas manufacture, he set out towards the thatched dwelling of the sheikh about the Mogareb.†

" The sheikh was sitting at his porch when Alee approached: he welcomed him kindly, and very graciously accepted his offerings.

" Alee, as I said, was fond of *somets*, and never had he been accused of passing the wooden bowl without taking a long and hearty pull. That night his potations were more deep and frequent than usual; and at length, overcome by the intoxicating fumes, the freebooter lay senseless on the floor.

" ' What sum has been offered for this drunkard?' said old Kador, the one-eyed, who, by-the-bye, had frequently handed the bowl to Alee (near to whom he had seated himself). ' They say,' he continued, ' that our lord the Sultan would give the dower of a Basha's daughter for the bullet-head of that villain. Are we to disregard the royal mandate? Are we to admit into our feasts one whose very hand is stained with the blood of our kindred? Did he not shoot my uncle's wife's brother, Kaid Moktar, while obeying the orders of Seeyedoona?‡ Are we to

* An intoxicating drink, being boiled juice of grape, which is distributed to the guests at the merry-makings of mountaineers in this country.
† The hour of evening prayer.
‡ Epithet for the Sultan, meaning " our Lord."

accept gifts bought at the price of blood ?. Are we, in the face
of God and man, to be a party to his lawless acts ? Let others
do as they please ; but I,' said he, unsheathing his dagger at the
same time, ' I will not be a traitor to my Sultan.' Heated with
wine, and excited by the appeal of the One-eyed, several of the
guests started up, applauding his decision. 'But,' said they,
' let us not take his life, and bring ill-luck upon the bride and
bridegroom ; rather let us secure his person, and send him in
chains to the Prince of Believers.'

"Now, knowing the immense strength of Alee, and his luck
in escaping from the hands of justice, they agreed, in order to
prevent any failure in their attempt, that two of the party should
be ready with loaded guns to shoot him if. he made the slightest
resistance.

"It was some moments before Alee discovered their treachery,
for the fumes of somets had addled his brains : resistance too
was useless, so he suffered himself to be bound hand and foot.

"Having effected this, the villagers called a consultation, and
agreed that three armed men should be left to watch him for
the night. Old Kador again interposed, saying, ' O fools ! ye
know not with whom you have to deal: this is not a thief of the
Shloh : this is not a cattle-stealer of Benimsooar. This is the
Six-fingered : ay, this is he for whom three hundred mitzakel
have been offered. If you will listen, I will tell you how to
secure him.'

" ' Speak then, O Kador,' they cried.

"Upon which the One-eyed said, ' Let the skin of his feet be
torn from the soles ; and then, if he break his bonds, he will not
have power to go far.'

"The savage proposition was put into execution. Alee groaned
with agony ; and called upon those around for mercy. To many
of them he had performed acts of kindness : but they had gone
too far to retract, and were deaf to his entreaties.

"This done, the three guards were left to watch their bleeding prisoner, who lay groaning with pain, the acuteness of which
had quite recovered him from his drunken fit.

"The night rolled on ; and the guards, tired of watching,
drowsy from the effects of wine, and trusting to the crippled
state of the robber, gave way to sleep : even old Kador, who

was one of their number, and the most watchful, thought he
might venture to snatch an hour of rest.

" On hearing the snoring of the guards, the hope of escape
flashed through the mind of Alee : but how to break his bonds
—for one or two efforts told him that even with his enormous
strength the thick palmetto cord was not to be conquered.

" Now, he remembered, there was a large flat slab of stone in
the centre of the hut, upon which the bowl of *somets* had been
placed, and the sides of which had been finely cut : so, creeping
towards it, he patiently rubbed the cord against the sharp edge
of the stone, until he had completely sawn through it, and his
hands became free.

" With a little dagger, which he cautiously removed from the
belt of one of the sleepers, he cut the cords that bound his feet :
then tearing off part of his turban, and creeping towards the
glimmering lamp, dipped the rags in the oil, and bound his mutilated feet. ' Now,' muttered he, ' I escape or die—but first let
me have revenge !' So, crawling towards the old Kador, the
cause of all his present suffering, he suddenly placed his iron fist
on the mouth of the old man, and with the other hand plunged
the dagger into his perfidious heart.

" ' Enough of blood,' said he, as he wiped his dagger : then
taking some loaves of bread in the hood of his jelabea, for he
reflected that in his state it would require many a long day to
reach his home, he crawled noiselessly out of the hut.

" All was quiet without—both dogs and men were alike overcome with the plentiful bounty of the sheikh : so, stealing along
snake-like through the village, he descended towards the river,
which at some half-mile from thence ran its rapid course towards
the sea.

" ' If,' cried Alee, ' God grant that I may reach the water,
then I yet may see my wife. Alas ! alas ! What will become
of Rahmana ? This day ought I to be in Sahel Forest.'

" The red tint of dawn had just risen from the east, when loud
cries of men and dogs resounded through the village. Alee
heard them, and his heart sunk within him : but the river was
now only distant some fifty yards ; he soon reached it, and having
quaffed a copious draught, he plunged into the stream, laying
flat on his back, and allowing the rapid current to carry him
whether it listed.

"The voices of his pursuers now approached, the baying of the dogs was heard nearer and nearer, and torches gleamed in every direction. Some of the villagers were mounted, others on foot; and all were armed with such weapons as had first come to hand, when their prisoner's escape had been announced.

" 'He cannot be far off,' said the foremost, 'for here are the traces of his knees; 'tis lucky his feet are useless, for the devil would not catch him were they sound.'

" 'And here is blood too,' said the son of old Kador the One-eyed—who, furious at his father's murder, swore to kill Alee with his own hand, though he himself had been one of the slumbering guards whom the freebooter had in mercy spared.

" 'By this track,' said another, 'he has clambered down the bank. See the marks of his cursed six fingers.'

" 'There is no God but God!' exclaimed a third: 'I will swear he is concealed among the oleanders. Hie, Zeitoon,' he said to his dog, who was giving tongue, hot on the tracks of blood.

" They now descended the bank, and found marks of their fugitive, down to the water's edge.

" 'He has passed the river!' was shouted out by many a voice, and then both men and horses dashed across the rapid stream. But no trace on the opposite bank could be found. They scoured the country all around—still they were at fault. 'He has paid the penalty of his crimes,' exclaimed one of them, 'and has been drowned while attempting to cross the river. May God have mercy on his soul!' and the party returned to the village.

" Alee, having floated a long way down the stream, and hearing nothing further of his pursuers, made for the shore, and lay some hours in the wet reeds, weak from loss of blood, excitement, and fatigue.

" During this time, however, he had dressed his wounds with the herb called Tserbil,* which grows in marshy ground, and which he had fortunately found near the water's edge, and its cooling qualities tended much to relieve his aching feet. As the evening set in, he again started on his painful journey, crawling on his knees and hands—which, after a few miles of such

* A kind of sage.

travelling, were reduced to almost as wretched a state as his mutilated feet—and he was again obliged to seek a hiding-place, until he could recover strength and heart to continue his journey.

" Thus did he labour on for five long days; and had it not been for the scraps of bread taken from the hut of the sheikh, he would have died of hunger. On the morning of the sixth day he reached his own hut. A horrid stillness prevailed; and a cold chill came over him, as with a trembling voice he called upon his wife: but no answer was returned. Alas, where was she who used to welcome the robber with tears of gladness? Again he called with a louder voice, 'Rahmana, where are you?' No reply gladdened his ear. Gasping for breath he entered the hut, and there lay the corpse of his poor wife, and on her cold bosom an infant dying from want of nourishment.

" 'Thy curse, O God, is on me,' he cried, 'and well have I deserved it! But why, O cruel fate, was I not permitted once again to see my wife while yet alive, and ask her forgiveness? And my poor child too—alas! alas!'

" Alee passed a long, long night of agony, bemoaning his cruel lot; upbraiding himself bitterly for the intemperance which had caused all this misery; and bathing with tears the remains of his beloved wife and child.

" The next day he peeled the bark from the trunk of a young cork-tree, and made a coffin for the bodies of his wife and child; vowing to bury them by the tomb of his patron saint,* in the wood of Sahel, as soon as his wounded feet would permit him to undertake the laborious task."

Notwithstanding the interest we all took in the fate of poor Alee, I could not help interrupting my friend the Arab, by asking him what was the employment of several ragged-looking mortals, who, half naked, were carrying large bundles through the wood. He told me they had been collecting bark, which had lately become an object of commerce at the port of Laraiche.

When we came up to these wretched specimens of humanity, they greeted me with the old rhyming malediction of " *Eusara*

---

* It is the custom of the Mahomedans to bury their dead near to the site where a saint has been interred.

fee senara, Lehood fee sefood" (the Christian to the hook, the Jew to the spit); upon which our escort, the valiant Mallem, was about to resent the insult, and, putting his Rozinante to the charge, would willingly have belaboured them with the long thong of his bridle (the horsewhip of Marocco), had not I checked his *generous* rage, to which he then gave vent in the following tirade:—"O naked scurvy dogs! O reptiles of the slime of the earth! Cover your shame and put a bridle to your tongues; look at these Nazarenes, God's own creatures, and reflect whether they or you are best fitted for the hook."

The Arab now continued his story. "Three weeks," he said, " had passed, and Alee's feet were much recovered; so, placing the bier upon his shoulders, and taking with him a fas,* he took his way to the sanctuary, which was a good six miles from his solitary abode; and there he buried the remains of her whom he had loved so dearly; and then he took an oath, over the fresh-dug grave, to abandon the life of a robber, and to visit daily, until death, the tomb of his lamented Rahmana. Being no longer provided with mòna by his friends, who all supposed him dead, and bound by oath not to commit violence, poor Alee subsisted on acorns, or such roots of the forest as he could procure; or else, crouching by the road-side with muffled face, begged bread, for the love of God, from the passers-by.

" Rumours now got abroad that a figure like that of the famous robber had often been seen sitting near the sanctuary of the Sahel wood; and orders came down from the court to the Kaid of Laraiche to inquire into the truth of these reports; and should Alee, the Six-fingered, be yet alive, and found to frequent the sanctuary, that he must be seized, and that even the sanctuary itself might be violated, should he take refuge there.

" It was Friday; Alee had taken a branch of myrtle, and was seated over the grave of his wife, speaking to her, after the Moorish fashion, as if yet alive. Wrapped in his thoughts, he did not perceive, until they were nigh upon him, some score of men, who now emerged from the wood, armed with guns. Alee was unarmed, for thus he always approached the holy ground: he had left his mare some way off in the wood, and his feet were not yet so much recovered as to be trusted to in flight: moreover he was tired of life, and cared not what became of himself;

* A large Moorish hoe.

so, walking leisurely towards the holy sepulchre, he entered therein.

"The soldiers now surrounded the sanctuary: it is a small coned building, within which is a framework of carved wood that covers the spot where the bones of the saint are laid.

"The orders were to bring the Six-fingered alive; so they agreed to surround the building, but not to commit any violence, unless Alee attempted to escape. Much discussion, however, ensued as to who should venture within to arrest the formidable culprit. At length three of the stoutest hearted agreed to undertake the bold adventure.

"Alee was sitting coiled up in a corner, his head bent to his knees, and his hands buried in the folds of his geelab.

"With fear and trembling the three armed men advanced a step; when Alee, raising his head and fixing his eagle eye on the foremost man, seized a huge stone, one of many which lay scattered in the tomb, and hurled it at his breast. The man fell, and the two others made off, but one of them, as he reached the threshold, was levelled by a second missile from the all-powerful hand of Alee.

"'And now,' exclaimed the Six-fingered, as he approached the door, 'no man shall lay hands on me within the sanctuary near to which my wife is laid; but I am sick of life, as all I cared for lies in yonder grave: so fear not,' said he to the Kaid of the troop, every man of which, with levelled gun, was expecting further mischief; 'take me prisoner, and convey me whithersoever you please.'

"He was now bound without offering resistance, and led out of the burial-ground.

"'*Aj Aj Mesòda*' (come here, Mesòda), cried the robber, as he reached the wood; and a moment afterwards a black mare, saddled and bridled, came neighing towards the party. The soldiers tried to catch her; but she reared and kicked, allowing no one to approach her. 'You had better leave *Mesòda* to me,' said the Six-fingered. The soldiers desisted from their endeavours to catch her, and the mare quietly approached her master. Alee now slipped the bridle from her head, kissed her face, and, giving her a light blow, cried '*Awa! Awa!*' and the mare, who seemed to understand his wishes, made off at full gallop into the wood.

" ' Go,' cried he, ' O pupil of my eye; no man shall ever possess you but in death! and thus indeed it would have been with thy master, had he not lost his mate.'

" Alee was taken prisoner to Laraiche, where the greater part of the population came forth to see the dreaded highwayman, and, as he passed, the curses of the many were showered on his doomed head, but they were intermingled with the blessings of not a few who recognised in him a former benefactor. Fetters were now riveted on his hands and feet, and a massive iron collar, with a chain that would have held a lion, was fastened round his neck. Thus secured, he was taken before the governor of the place, who ordered him to be lodged in a dungeon.

" The sultan, having been apprised of the robber's arrest, issued a royal letter, declaring him an outlaw, and condemning him to lose the right hand and the right foot; that then he should be released, and allowed to limp about as a moral lesson for others of like character.

" On the day appointed for the execution of this dreadful sentence, Alee was led forth to the market-place, where crowds of people had assembled from all the country around to witness the fate of him who had been the cause of such terror to this western world.

" The executioner was ready with his knife, and near at hand was placed a bowl of hot pitch, wherein the stumps were to be thrust to stop the bleeding. His manacles, as I have told you, had been riveted on, and a blacksmith was about to be summoned to break them off, when Alee exclaimed, ' Is it for these toys you require a blacksmith?' and, jerking back his hands, he snapped them asunder.

" His right hand was now seized by the executioner, who, with three other men, endeavoured to force it from the socket previous to cutting it off at its joint. ' Why do you tremble?' said Alee to the executioner; ' give me the knife, and I will do what you dare not. Fear not that I shall use the knife against you: my doom is sealed; and had I so wished, I would have escaped long ago.' The knife was given to him, and, the four men pulling at his hand, he with his left hand severed it with one cut, and plunged the bleeding stump into the boiling pitch without a groan. His foot was then amputated by the executioner, and then the poor wretch was abandoned to his fate.

" Two days after, Alee Boofrahee, the Champion, the Six-fingered, was found dead, lying on the grave of Rahmana. He is said to have expired raving mad, and was buried by some charitable persons near to the body of his wife.

" May God have mercy on their souls ! " said the Arab, and ended the tale.

It may be here remarked, that notwithstanding the tyrannical laws of this country, capital punishments are very rare; and, during the last ten years, three only have taken place in the town of Tangier. On one of those occasions I was unintentionally present.

I had risen at break of day, and, accompanied by a friend, had set out to shoot near the town, in ignorance of the execution which was about to take place. On reaching the principal gate of the town, we found it shut, which surprised us much, knowing old Ben Khajjr, the porter, to be an early riser. We then proceeded to the castle gate, called Bab Marshen, which was also shut, but Ben Khajjr was there, with a multitude of people, who, like ourselves, were desirous to leave the town.

" Why are you so late to-day? " said I to the old porter. Ben Khajjr replied in enigmas; he had his orders not to let any Mussulmen pass outside the gate for the next half-hour.

" Surely," I said, " your instructions do not extend to us. If there has been a robbery in the town—to which alone I can attribute this unusual order—we are not likely to be the persons."

" Well," said the old gatekeeper, as I slipped into his hand a small silver key, " you and your friend may pass, but no Moor can."

We sallied forth, wondering what could be the cause of such a novel order. This, however, was soon explained; for the first object that caught our eye was a party of soldiers moving slowly down the road adjoining the old ditch on the south-western side of the town wall.

As we hastened towards the party, we perceived they had two prisoners, who were secured with ropes fastened round their arms and waist. I recognised one of them to be a native of Reef, who had formerly been a gardener in the service of one of my friends at Tangier. He was a fine, tall, handsome youth, and his countenance was far from indicating anything vicious and depraved.

Having joined them, I inquired of the kaid of the soldiers what was the cause of these men being led as prisoners.

"The Sultan—may God prolong his life!" said he, "has ordered that their heads be cut off; they have been carrying on a contraband trade in oxen on the coast of Reef with the infidel Spaniard."

"This, indeed," I replied, "is a severe punishment for such a crime : and if it be intended as a warning to others, why prevent the people of Tangier from witnessing it?"

"Reason not with me, Nazarene," said the kaid; "I have my orders, and shall soon obey them."

The Jewish slaughter-ground had been selected as the spot for the execution. There we found a depraved-looking Moor dressed as a butcher, holding in his hand a small knife about half a foot long. This man, we were informed, was the executioner; he was a stranger, and had been hired to act on this occasion; for the Mahomedan butchers of Tangier, who are the persons constrained to perform such service when a regular executioner cannot be found, had taken refuge in the sanctuary of Mesmoody; and had it not been for this person offering his services, the authorities would have been much perplexed how to obey the mandate of the sultan; though the commander of the troops, when informed by the governor of the difficulty, drew his sword, and exclaimed, "Let the criminals be brought to me, and I shall always be found ready to execute the orders of the Prince of Believers, be they what they may."

A morbid curiosity chained me to the spot, although I foresaw that I should have to witness a most horrid scene.

Some wrangling now ensued between the kaid's soldiers and the executioner as to the reward which the latter was to receive for decapitating the poor wretches; who, all the time, were standing by, compelled to listen to this bartering for their blood. The butcher insisted that four dollars had been offered him for one head alone, and that he must have a second four for the other. The kaid unwillingly yielded the point, and immediately the first victim, who was already half dead with terror, was thrown down on the ground by the executioner, who, kneeling on his breast, put the knife to his throat. I turned away, a violent struggle ensued, and I heard the executioner say, "Give me another knife; mine won't cut." I looked round; the wretched man was lying with his throat half cut, his breast heaving, and every limb writhing! My companion now loudly reproached the party for their cold-blooded atrocity, and called upon them to put the suffering man out of his misery. After a time another knife was handed by a soldier to the executioner, and the head was severed.

The soldiers shouted feebly "May God prolong the life of our Sultan!" though I observed that many of them were as much horrified as ourselves.

I remained riveted on the spot, where yet another victim awaited his fate. This was the fine-looking fellow of whom I have spoken: again there took place a bartering for his blood; the kaid denying his late promise, and declaring that he would not give even the four dollars unless the head of the second criminal was cut off. To this the executioner was at length forced to consent. The culprit now begged to be untied. This request being acceded to, he took off his geelab, and giving it to the soldier who had performed this last act of kindness towards him, said "Accept this; we shall yet meet in another world." His turban he threw to another, who had uttered a word of pity, instead of joining in the insulting shout of the soldiery; and walking steadily to the spot where his companion lay, he cried out with a distinct voice, "There is no God but God, and Mahomed is his prophet." Then turning to the executioner, he loosened his girdle, and gave it to him, saying, "For the love of God, sever my head with better dispatch than you did that of my brother." He laid himself flat on the ground, yet moist with blood; and the knee of the ruffian, for so he deserved to be called, was placed on the Reefian's breast. A horseman was now seen galloping towards the party.

"A reprieve!" shouted my friend. "Stop! stop!" The executioner withheld his knife.

"It is only the son of the governor," exclaimed a soldier; "he is coming to see the execution. Wait for him."

I rushed away in horror; and soon afterwards we saw the soldiers bearing in their hands the two bleeding heads.

As we felt no desire to continue our walk, we waited with the soldiers till the gates were opened. A fresh dispute took place between them and the executioner, who demanded protection from the populace, which the soldiers refused to give, unless he gave them two dollars, the half of his earnings. This the butcher refused to do, and he was left to his fate.

No sooner had the gates been opened than a troop of boys had rushed out and attacked the executioner with stones. The man fled into the country, pursued by the young mob, and it was reported that he had fallen senseless some three miles from the town, covered with a hundred bruises.

On entering the town the soldiers seized the first Jew they met, and obliged him to salt the heads, which were subsequently hung from the top of a square tower on the town wall, fronting the great market-place.

As I returned homeward I met in the little sokh a Reefian, whom I knew to be a cousin of the deceased gardener, armed with a brace of pistols and a dagger, hurrying along. On asking him what was the matter, he replied, " I am about to revenge the death of my relation on that cursed stranger, who alone was found ready to cause our blood to flow."

Next day there was a report that the executioner had been shot, and buried on the spot. No inquiry appeared to have been made by the authorities at Tangier, for the cousin returned, and remained unmolested.

After three days' exposure, the heads were sent to the Sultan, to convince his imperial majesty that his orders had been obeyed: they were met on the road by a courier bringing a reprieve, who was said to have been detained in consequence of one of the rivers having been swollen from heavy rains.

Another instance of capital punishment was attended with the following singular circumstances. A Moor of the village of Sharf had shot with a pistol in the market at Tangier a fellow-villager, whom he suspected of being too intimate with his wife. The brother of the murdered man set out immediately for Meknas, where the Sultan was then residing, and claimed the life of the murderer. The Sultan heard the case, acknowledged the justice of the demand, and summoning the plaintiff into his presence, delivered the following curious decision :—

" We grant you our permission to take the life of the murderer of your brother with the same instrument of death with which he was assassinated, and on the same spot, and at the same hour of the day. But," added the Sultan, " why seekest

thou also to be a manslayer? Accept the price of blood, which
is lawful unto true believers, and we will guarantee you its pay-
ment from our Shereefian hands, and two hundred mitzakel shall
be the sum."

To this the plaintiff replied, " Can that sum purchase me a
brother? "

" Go thy way," said the Sultan ; " we have heard and understood : a letter will be given you by the vizier, in which our
mandate shall be written."

Furnished with the sentence of death, the man returned to
Tangier, and presented it to the governor.

On the same day of the week, and at the same hour, the murderer was brought out of prison, and seated on the very spot
where he had taken his fellow-villager's life, while crowds of
people attended to witness his death.

The pistol was now given to the brother of the murdered
man : when, having loaded it, he went up to the criminal, walked
slowly in a circle round him, and said, " In the presence of God
and man, I call upon you to answer me truly. Didst thou slay
my brother? "

To this the criminal replied, " I did."

One of the multitude, now stepping forward, addressed the
brother of the murdered man : " Accept the price of blood,"
said he, " and I promise you one hundred ducats in addition,
which those here assembled will gladly give."

" Worthless words," said the villager ; and again he walked
round his victim. Again he asked him the same question, and
again the same reply was given. A second offer was now made,
of two hundred ducats ; and again the villager, walking round
the criminal, repeated his question, adding, " Say what thou
believest ; I am about to take thy life."

" That God is God, and Mahomed is the prophet of God ! "
responded the criminal.

Hardly were these words out of his mouth, when the pistol
was discharged. It had been placed at the small of his back,
being the same spot where he had shot the man for whom he
was now about to die ; but the wretched criminal, although mor-
tally wounded, did not expire for some hours.

CHAPTER IX.

River Al Kous—Moorish Squadron—Sallee Rovers—Maniacs—Ferry—Laraiche—The Palacio—Basha's Message—The Market-place—Story of the Clockmaker—Scarcity of Provisions—Snake-Charmers—Jewish Fanaticism—A Hebrew Bride—Legend of the Sea and Gnats.

ERE the owner of the "rat-tailed" had concluded his story of Alee Boofrahee, our party had emerged from the wood of Sahel, and before us stood the town of Laraiche; its meandering river Al Kous lay below in its curious coils, like a glassy serpent lurking in the valley.

Having traversed a sandy and sterile soil for above three miles, we descended to that part of the river where the imperial squadron lay in ordinary; and less than *ordinary* they were, consisting in all of a corvette, two brigs, once merchant-vessels, which had been bought of the Christians, and a schooner, with some few gun-boats; and all of them, I was assured by sailors, were unfit for sea. Anchors, sails, and ropes were lying in a state of decay along the bank of the river. Such was the sorry remnant of the naval force of Marocco, whose Sallee rovers used to keep in constant alarm the peaceful merchantmen of Christendom. The terror they once inspired would appear not yet to have lost all its influence upon some maritime states, although the spirit and the power of those rovers are utterly defunct; for two nations, famed deservedly for their sea-kings of the north, and possessing gallant navies, continue, through some curious policy, or out of veneration, it may be, for olden custom, to pay annually a large and disgraceful tribute to the Moorish potentate, as if he were still the formidable toll-keeper of the Herculean straits.

Shortly after we had passed the sultan's arsenal, we were met by a disgusting but not unfrequent spectacle in Marocco; it was a sainted maniac, naked as on the day of his birth, except a party-coloured sackcloth, which covered his shoulders and back, his hair was long and matted, and his beard extended to the middle of his breast; in his hand he carried a short spear orna-

mented with plates of brass and bits of red cloth. On approaching him our attendants dismounted, and bowing their heads,
seized his hand and kissed it. My turn came next: and as I did
not like to come to such close quarters, I threw him a small
piece of money; upon which the poor creature jabbered some
few words of thanks, and then stalking up to me with all the
dignity of a basha, and an air of condescending patronage,
seized the collar of my coat and spat upon my eyes. I knew
enough of the habits of the people to be aware that this was a
high compliment, but I could not restrain myself from making
a wry face upon the occasion; and I was pulling out my handkerchief to wipe off the filth, when the Mallem cried out, " O
blessed Nazarene, what God has given let not man efface. Thou
shalt be happy! Seedy Momoh, the inspired, has spat upon
thee. Thou shalt be happy!" There is no use running in the
teeth of superstition, so the holy spittle dried on my face.

The madman or idiot is universally looked upon in West
Barbary as a person to be held in reverence. The Moor tells
you that God has retained their reason in heaven, whilst their
body is on earth; and that when madmen or idiots speak, their
reason is for the time permitted to return to them, and that their
words should be treasured up as those of inspired persons. These
wretched people are allowed to parade the streets in a state of
nudity, and the maniacs sometimes prove most dangerous to
unwary Europeans. A French consul-general some years ago
was nearly killed by a sainted madman, and in 1830 I had a
very narrow escape for my life from another.

I happened to be walking on the sea-shore with my sister immediately below the walls of the town of Tangier, when I espied
above us a wild-looking fellow about seventy or eighty yards off,
with a clotted head of hair that bespoke a sainted madman, aiming at me with his long gun, which he had rested on the wall.
We were near a rock at the time, behind which we took refuge,
and waited there a good while, in the hope that the madman's
patience would be worn out; but he did not stir, and the passers
by, whom I appealed to for their interference, shook their heads,
muttered something about Seedy Tayeb, which proved to be the
name of the saint, and went their way. In the meantime the
tide was rising rapidly, and we had the unpleasant choice of being

drowned or shot. We agreed it was better to risk the latter; so telling my sister to run off in another direction, I stepped forward and gave him the preference of a standing shot. The maniac took aim and fired; and I heard the ball whiz into the water behind me. I was proceeding to run up to him by a path which led to that part of the town wall where he was standing, when I observed that he was coolly reloading his gun; and as the next shot at close quarters might have proved more effective, I thought the best thing I could do was to follow my sister; so I fairly took to my heels.

Having reached home, and described to our guard the appearance of the man, we were sallying out to seize him, when the maniac himself, Seedy Tayeb, rushed into our court-yard, laughing heartily, and presented me with a basket of melons. The poor fellow was a most confirmed madman, and consequently a very great saint: and as I had not the heart to proceed formally against him, I only required that he should be imprisoned until he could be sent to the interior, whence the governor of Tangier promised he should not return.

But to return to our journey. After proceeding a short distance we reached the ferry; and except that of Charon, there can scarcely be one more perilous to cross. There is no pier, nor is there a plank provided to accommodate either man or beast in embarking.

A boisterous scene of whipping, kicking, and rearing now ensued, as is usual here; and broken knees or other more serious injuries are the frequent result, before a timid horse can be made to take the awkward leap, or be dragged by main force over the high side of the clumsy craft. My horse refused at first to make the leap, but having myself got into the boat and caressed the intelligent animal, he cleared the gunwale at a bound, and poking his muzzle into my lap, seemed to say—*Now that I have obeyed your wishes, I look to you for protection.*

The ferry is in the hands of government; an impudent negro and a lazy Moor were the boat's crew. Having struggled through the stream, we landed in the same awkward style under the town wall, amongst a rabble of Jew porters, who, like their European brethren, contend and clamour for your baggage, till the strongest carry it off by main force.

There were trading vessels, British, French, and Spanish, moored at the mouth of the river, waiting for cargoes; which consist principally of wool, skins, bark, beans, and grain of various sorts, which are taken in return for iron, broadcloth, cottons, muslin, sugar, and tea.

We rode through the gate of Laraiche followed by an insolent mob, to whom we gave full permission to curse and swear at the Nazarenes whilst they were out of our hearing; but I deemed it expedient now and then to warn them of the Basha's displeasure, if any one dared " to burn my grandfather."* The very name of Eslowy caused their grim faces to assume a ghastly smile at the Kaffer † who could obtain the protection of their dreaded governor.

We reached our consular agent's *palacio*, as the Jews dwelling upon the coast of this country, whose ancestors were exiled from the Spanish peninsula some three hundred years ago, still call their wretched habitations. The British agent, a native Jew, had provided for us two of his best rooms. There were, for a wonder, windows in one of them; but of glass, of course, there was none. However, we had two chairs and a carpet, which were the sole, yet unusually ample, furniture. We longed for our tent and the fresh air of the country; but we should have caused a mighty hubbub in the town, had we encamped outside its walls, instead of accepting apartments in the *Palacio del Consul Ingles*. In the street before my lodging were the remains of large houses that had evidently been at one time the decent and comfortable dwellings of European consuls, when Laraiche was the residence of several representatives of Christian states in this country; but these habitations were now far too ruinous and filthy for us to hazard the taking up our abode within their walls.

Shortly after my arrival I sent a message to the Basha with many salams, asking an audience of his excellency for the following day. A soldier soon presented himself, bidding me welcome in the great man's name, and appointing my interview with him at ten the next morning. With usual Moorish effrontery the messenger demanded of me a fee for conveying the Basha's

* A common curse in West Barbary.
† The rebeller against God.

wishes, which he told me were worth a doubloon.*   On offering a suitable gift, he refused it, as not being equal to his expectation ; so I threw it to a beggar who had been dinning us with a tale of woe, telling him that he had to thank the impudence of the soldier for this godsend.   The contrast between the messenger's face and that of the beggar was well worth the trifle.

Before the day closed, we took a stroll towards the marketplace, which is a broad and handsome street, having on one side a colonnade, and on the other the ruins of a Portuguese church, and of several handsome mansions, evidently of Christian architecture.   The principal mosque is a fine building, but its minaret, as is frequently the case in these Saracenic structures, appears too slim and lofty for its base.

We were careful not to excite the displeasure of the inhabitants by halting before the entrance to have a peep into the interior ; for the Moors, unlike their partially enlightened brethren of the East, prohibit the Christian and the Jew from entering a mosque or other place consecrated by the law of the Prophet, under pain of death, or embracing the faith of Islam.   A droll instance of this occurred some years ago at Tangier.

The clock of the " *Jamaa Kebeer*," the great mosque at Tangier, being much out of order, needed some skilful craftsman to repair it.   None, however, of the " Faithful" were competent to the task, nor could they even discover what part of the machinery was deranged, though many put forth their opinions with great pomp and authority ; amongst the rest one man gravely declared that a *Jin*, or evil genius, had in all probability taken up its abode within the clock.   Various exorcisms were accordingly essayed, sufficient, as every true believer supposed, to have expelled a legion of devils—yet all in vain : the clock continued dumb.

A Christian clockmaker, " a cursed Nazarene," was now their sole resource ; and such a one fortunately was sojourning in Tangier—" the city protected of the Lord."   He was from Genoa, and of course a most pious Christian ; how then were they, the faithful followers of the Prophet, to manage to employ him? The clock was fixed in the wall of the tower, and it was, of

---

* A gold coin worth sixteen Spanish dollars

course, a thing impossible to allow the Kaffer to defile God's house of prayer by his sacrilegious steps.

The time-keeper *Moakheed* reported the difficulty to the kady ;* and so perplexed the grey-bearded dealer in law and justice by the intricacy of the case, that, after several hours of deep thought, the judge confessed he could not come to a decision, and proposed to report upon the subject to the kaid, advising that a meeting of the local authorities should be called. "For, in truth," said the kady, "I perceive that the urgency of this matter is great. Yes! I myself will expound our dilemma to the kaid."

The kaid entered feelingly into all the difficulty of the case, and forthwith summoned the other authorities to his porch, where various propositions were put forward by the learned members of the council.

One proposed to abandon the clock altogether; another would lay down boards over which the infidel might pass without touching the sacred floor; but this was held not to be a sufficient safeguard; and it was finally decided to pull up that part of the pavement on which the Kaffer trod, and whitewash the walls near which he passed.

The Christian was now sent for, and told what was required of him; and he was expressly commanded to take off his shoes and stockings on entering the Jamaa. "That I won't," said the stout little watchmaker; "I never took them off when I entered the chapel of the most Holy Virgin," and here he crossed himself devoutly, "and I won't take them off in the house of your Prophet."

They cursed in their hearts the watchmaker and all his race, and were in a state of vast perplexity. The wise Oolama † had met early in the morning; it was already noon, and yet, so far from having got over their difficulty, they were in fact exactly where they had been before breakfast; when a grey-bearded Mueddin, who had hitherto been silent, craved permission to speak. The kaid and the kady nodded their assent.

"If," said the venerable priest, "the mosque be out of repair, and lime and bricks have to be conveyed into the interior for the use of the masons, do not asses carry those loads, and do not they enter with their shoes on?"

* Judge.   † Learned men.

" You speak truly," was the general reply.

" And does the donkey," resumed the Mueddin, " believe in the One God, or in Mahomed the Prophet of God ?"

" No, in truth," all replied.

" Then," said the Mueddin, " let the Christian go in shod as a donkey would do, and come out like a donkey."

The argument of the Mueddin was unanimously applauded. In the character of a donkey, therefore, did the Christian enter the Mahomedan temple, mended the clock—not indeed at all like a donkey—but as such, in the opinion of " the Faithful," came out again; and the great mosque of Tangier has never since needed another visit of the donkey to its clock.

There appeared to be in the market a great scarcity of all sorts of provisions, considering the population, which, I suppose, may amount to about 3000 souls—and my servants complained of much difficulty in finding food for either ourselves or our cattle.

As we strolled through the market-place we met a party of Eisowy, or snake-charmers; they consisted of four Soosys, or natives of the province of Soos ; three of whom were musicians, their instruments being long rude canes resembling in form a flute, but open at both ends, into one of which the performer blew, producing melancholy but pleasing notes.

We invited the Eisowy to exhibit their snakes; to this they readily assented. They commenced by raising up their hands as if they were holding a book, muttering in unison a prayer addressed to the Deity, and calling upon Seedna* Eiser, who in Marocco is held as the patron saint of snake-charmers. Having concluded this invocation, the music struck up, and the snake-charmer danced in rapid whirls, which no Strauss could have kept time to, around the basket containing the reptiles. This basket was made of cane-work covered with goat's skin. Stop-

---

* This is quite a distinct personage from Seedna Aisa, which is the name given by the Arabs to our Saviour. Christ is also called the *Roh Allah*, or " Breath of God." The Arabs do not believe in the crucifixion of our Saviour; they suppose that a man resembling Christ was miraculously placed in his stead whilst he ascended to heaven. I am told there was a law in Marocco to punish with death by fire any Mahomedan cursing Seedna Aisa. The Moors hold both the Old and New Testament in veneration, but say that these divine works were superseded by the Koran. They also tell us that we possess garbled copies of the inspired authors, as no mention is found in them of the coming of the Prophet Mahomed.

ping suddenly, the snake-charmer thrust his bare arm into the basket, and pulled out a large black Cobra Capella, or hooded snake: this he handled as if it had been his turban, and proceeded to twine it around his head, dancing as before, whilst the reptile seemed to obey his wishes, by preserving its position on his head. The Cobra was then placed on the ground, and standing erect on its tail moved its head to and fro, apparently keeping time to the music. Now, whirling round in circles still more rapidly than before, the Eisowy again put his hand into the basket and pulled out successively and placed on the ground two very poisonous species of serpents, natives of the deserts of Soos, called Leffa. They were of a mottled colour with black spots; were thick in the body and not above two feet and a half or three feet long.* The name Leffa is given, I imagine, by the Mogrebbin Arabs to this kind of serpent, from their resemblance, when in the act of darting at their prey, to the Arabic letter ڢ, fa,† le being merely the article transposed. These reptiles proved more active and less docile than the Cobra; for half coiled and holding their heads in a slanting position ready for an attack, they watched with sparkling eyes the movements of the charmer, darting at him with open jaws every now and then, as he ventured within their reach, and throwing forward their body with amazing velocity, whilst their tail appeared to remain on the same spot, and then recoiling back again. The Eisowy warded off with his long haik the attacks which they made upon his bare legs, and the Leffas seemed to expend their venom upon the garment.

Now, calling on Seedna Eiser, he seized hold of one of the two serpents by the nape of the neck, and danced round with it; then opening its jaws with a small stick, he displayed to the spectators the fangs, from which there oozed a white and oily substance. He then put the Leffa to his arm, which it immediately seized with its teeth, whilst the man, making hideous contortions, as if in pain, whirled rapidly around, calling on his patron saint. The reptile continued its bite until the Eisowy took it off, and showed us the blood which it had drawn.

Having laid the Leffa down, he then put the bitten part of his

---

* A sketch of these reptiles is given in Aly Beg's work on Marocco.

† In the East the fa is written thus ڢ; the point being put above, instead of below the letter.

arm into his mouth; and, pressing it with his teeth, danced for several minutes, whilst the music played more rapidly than ever, till, apparently being quite exhausted, he again halted.

Conceiving that the whole was a trick—that the Leffa had been bereft of its poison, and that its bite consequently would be as harmless as that of a rat, I requested to be allowed to handle the serpent.

" Are you an Eisowy?" said the man of Soos; " or have you steady faith in the power of our saint?"

I replied in the negative.

" Then," said he, " if the snake bite you, your hour is come! Bring me a fowl or any animal, and I will give you sure proof, ere you attempt to touch a Leffa."

A fowl was brought, and part of the feathers having been plucked, the serpent was again taken up by the charmer, and allowed to bite the fowl for an instant. The bird was put on the ground, and after running around as if in a fit for about the space of a minute, tottered and fell dead. Its flesh became shortly afterwards of a bluish hue. It is needless to say that after this I declined handling the Leffa.

The only way that I can account for the Eisowy escaping unharmed from the bite of the snake, is, that either he prevents the Leffa, when in the act of seizing his arm, from using *its* *fangs*, and that the blood seen is drawn by the teeth only of the reptile, which are distinct from its fangs, or else that the Eisowy possesses an antidote to the poison, and that he puts it into his mouth and applies it to the bitten part during the dance.

Putting these serpents into the basket, the snake-charmer next took out some common snakes caught in the neighbourhood of Tangier, amongst which I observed the *Boomenfakh*, or " *father of tumefaction:*" the bite of these snakes is not in general of so venomous a nature as to endanger life. The Eisowy played with them for some time, and allowed them to bite his half-naked body whilst he danced around streaming with blood; then taking the tail of one of them into his mouth, whilst others twined themselves around his body, he commenced eating, or rather chewing, the reptile; which, writhing with pain, bit him in the neck and hands until it was actually destroyed by the Eisowy's teeth:—a most cruel and disgusting sight.

I have frequently witnessed individuals belonging to the sect of Eisowys, in whose company I have chanced to be during my sporting expeditions, handle scorpions or poisonous reptiles without fear or injury, the animal never attempting to sting or bite them. Whilst I was residing at Tangier, a young Moor, who was witnessing the exploits of a snake-charmer, ridiculed his prowess as a mere delusion, and having been dared by the Eisowy to touch one of his serpents, the lad ventured into the mystic ring, was bitten by a Leffa, and shortly afterwards expired.

Seedna Eiser is said to have lived about two centuries ago, and to have been a very learned man and a preacher of the Unity of God. It is related of this personage that whilst travelling through the Desert of Soos, he was followed by a great multitude, who thirsted for the precepts which dropped like precious jewels from the mouth of the sage, and as the multitude travelled afar, they hungered and clamoured to Seedna Eiser for bread. On this the sage's patience forsook him, and turning around to the multitude, he exclaimed in a voice of rebuke, " *Kool sim* "— a common Arabic curse which means " Eat poison." The saint's followers, taking these words literally, treasured them up in their hearts, and having unbounded faith in their efficacy, they fed upon the reptiles of the desert, and were preserved from hunger and exhaustion; and from that time, their descendants, and all those who believe in Seedna Eiser's power, handle without fear or injury the most poisonous reptiles.

The individuals of this sect, of which there are many in most of the towns throughout West Barbary, resemble in some respects the jumping Dervishes of the East, assembling, like them, on certain feast-days, in houses appropriated for the purpose, and there celebrating the rites of their faith. They conceive that their love and reverence for their patron and saint arrive at so high a pitch as to surpass the bounds of man's reason, and this creates for the time in which they indulge in their worship an aberration of the senses, which causes them to suppose that they become wild animals, such as lions, tigers, dogs, birds, &c., and they commence roaring, barking, and imitating both the voice and action of whatever animal they may have taken a fancy to be changed into; tearing themselves and each other. This state of madness is partly brought on by an intoxicating herb called hasbeesh, which is swallowed in small quantities and a glass of water taken to wash it down; or by smoking keek, likewise a herb found in Marocco. When the Eisowys are in this state, they are sometimes paraded through the streets chained or bound together, and preceded by their *Emkadem*, or chief, on horseback. They utter the most horrible sounds and leap about in every direction. A live sheep is sometimes thrown to them by the spectators; this they will tear and devour in the raw state, entrails and all.

If they happen to break away from their fetters, they will seize upon any Jew or Christian whom they meet. Not many years ago, in Tangier, a Jewish boy was said to have been torn to pieces; but I am not inclined to believe that such horrid cruelty could exist even in West Barbary.

On one occasion I was attacked by one of these individuals, who had broken away from his companions; but having with me a thick stick, which I applied very energetically to his bare skull, it seemed to awaken his reasoning faculties, for he left me and commenced devouring some cabbages in a shop hard by.

The Moors look upon these sects with a less favourable eye than the Turks, for individuals of high importance of the latter race are often enrolled among the Dervishes.

It has often occurred to me that these rites, which appear so repugnant to the laws of the Prophet, must be the remains of some more ancient worship, and that in the mystic dance of the Dervishes may be traced a remnant of the solar worship, the movements of the performers being typical of the revolutions of the heavenly bodies.

We returned to our hovel just in time to enjoy a splendid view from its windows of a sunset on the verge of the broad Atlantic. Then dinner being announced, our host joined us at table, and, being a Rabbi, went through the usual forms and prayers in cutting bread and pouring out the wines, and on sitting down and rising up; all which looked much like *hocus pocus* to our "heathen" minds. It was the Sabbath-eve, and he could not touch fire nor hold a lighted candle. To such an extent, indeed, does this superstition prevail among these benighted children of

Israel, that a poor young woman whose clothes had caught fire on a Saturday, and this in the midst of her family, among whom were several grown-up men, was obliged to rush into the street, and would have been burnt to death had it not been for the prompt assistance of some passing Moslem.

Our host proved to be an intelligent and cunning Jew. His wife was dead; and two wretched-looking children, the only pledges of affection his late spouse had left him, were intrusted to the care of his sister, an elderly matron, who might perhaps some twenty years ago have boasted of good looks. The Jewesses of Marocco are for the most part a comely race, especially those of Tetuan, who, I have thought, sometimes rivalled in regularity of features even my own dear countrywomen—the fairest of the fair: but in expression the uneducated Jewess of Barbary disappoints her Christian admirer; there is nothing intellectual about her, and she is, in truth, merely a beautiful animal.

While at dinner, our meal and talk were interrupted by the noise of a cymbal and the shrill yell of women, accompanied by the nasal shouts of the Hebrew tribe, who were conducting a bride to her betrothed; the procession stopped beneath our window, as a compliment to the strangers, who might wish to see the finery of the happy damsel. She was, indeed, extremely pretty, and fair as purest wax: her "Jew's eyes" were shut, but the eyelashes and eyebrows were all a bridegroom could wish. A blaze of torches surrounded her, and she was supported by her male relations. Every muscle of her countenance seemed immoveably fixed, in obedience to the rigid ordinances of her race; and the poor bride looked, as she proceeded on her way, more like an automaton than a living lass just about to be married. On her head was a tiara rich in pearls and other jewelry. Her dress was of crimson and gold cloth; and a necklace, bracelets, and anklets of a very antique form loaded her slender person.* Her feet were *stockingless*, but were encased in gilded leathern shoes. Don José and myself made audible

---

* Even the poorest classes in Marocco wear on holidays apparel of the richest kind. Their jewelry is often very ancient, being handed down from mother to daughter from time immemorial.

vows for her happiness, and then she was led on to the dwelling of her future lord.

Although the Jews of this country are ruled by their Mahomedan masters with the extremest tyranny, and are constantly treated with the most shameful injustice, their importance to the welfare of the state seems to be fully understood; for the government has imposed a legal check on their emigration, by prohibiting the embarkation for another country of any female of the Jewish persuasion. The gold, silver, and tin smiths are mostly Jews; and much more than half of the principal traders in the seaport towns of Marocco are of the Hebrew nation.

Dinner being over, our host and his sister retired; and my fellow-traveller, wrapped in his *capa* and stretched on the carpet, was soon heard snoring in deep sleep, whilst I, seated on the ground after the fashion of a Moorish scribe, wrote my journal till the expiring flame of my lamp put an end to my further lucubration, and I settled myself to sleep as composedly as I could. But my rest was most abominably invaded by every possible variety of noisome insects, amongst which the gnats were the most unendurable. Anything worthy of the name of sleep was out of the question: and when, as the morning dawned, my friend the Hadj entered our apartment, and inquired how we had passed our first night at Laraiche, I broke out into a violent philippic against the place and all its inhabitants, the gnats especially; and ended by expressing my astonishment that such detestable animals should ever have been created.

The Hadj appeared greatly shocked at my impiety. "Mashallah!" (the will of God) ejaculated he with reverence. "All things were made by God for some good purpose: and now, Christian, you shall learn of me the history of the gnat.

"In the beginning God created the sea, and in his goodness made it sweet, even as the waters of the living fountain. And God appointed a vast extent for its dominion, and endowed it with wondrous power above all his other creatures. Then the sea, raising his head to the stars and roaring terribly, lashed the borders of the land and terrified mankind; and growing day by day more arrogant, it abused in wantonness the power given it, and, passing the limits given it by its Creator, overwhelmed the land, and, destroying every living thing that was on the face of the earth, hearkened no more to the rebukes of its Maker. And man and all God's creatures, excepting the fish, sought in vain for refuge, and were drowned in the whirlpool of its fury.

"Then God spake unto the sea and said, 'Hear, O sea! thou hast laughed to scorn thy Creator; and not hearkening to my voice, thou hast overleaped the limits that I ordained for thee: wherefore, lo! I will now create the most insignificant of winged insects, and I will create them in countless myriads, and thou shalt know that I am thy master and thy God.' So God created the gnat. And clouds of gnats darkened the face of the earth. And God said unto the gnats, 'Settle ye on the face of the sea, and drink thereof.' And the gnats drank; and the sea became dry; yea, the terrible sea became as nothing in the stomach of the puny gnat. And now God spake thus unto the sea as it lay in the stomach of the gnats, and said, 'Know ye, now, O sea! that I am the Lord of all.' And the sea repented and acknowledged Him to be the Lord. And God said unto the gnats, 'Vomit up now the waters from your stomachs.' And the gnats did as God commanded; and the sea returned unto its bed; but the waters thereof became salt, owing to the stomach of the gnats; and thus God ordained that it should remain, that the sea might know that He is the Lord, and that there is none other God."*

"Wondrous and miraculous," I exclaimed, "are the ways of God! The gnat, in truth, is a wily insect. Hark ye, now, O Hadj, how he tunes his pipe, buzzing sweetly, '*Habeeby! Habeeby!*' (O my beloved! O my beloved!), and while thus fascinating us with his charms, he suddenly stoops; and, brute as he is, darts his relentless sting into the object of his admiration. There, I have killed one! and, O sea! I am thy avenger."

* This legend is, I believe, peculiar to the Berber tribes. It is evidently formed on the Mosaic account of the deluge.

CHAPTER X.

Visit to the Basha—Scene in an Arab Dooar—Arab Resignation—Visit to
a Synagogue—The Sacred Scrolls—The High Priest—Battery—A gifted
Cannon—Christian Cemetery—Town Walls—History of Mulai Yezeed—
A Moorish Cart—Policy of the Sultan—The Basha's Favourite—Eating
up a Province—Human Sacrifice—Manner of crossing a River.

AT the appointed hour, preceded by Mallem Hamed and a
soldier from the Basha, we paced with measured steps to the
Kasba, or citadel, wherein is situated the "*Dar-al-Kebeer*,"*
the residence of the governor. Having passed through an ancient Moorish archway, we were desired to stop near a mosque,
that notice might be given to the great man of our approach.
The messenger soon returned, bidding us move on. Again we
were brought to a halt in the porch, in front of which were the
guard, *seated*, as is usual in Marocco, unless when the governor
himself, or some personage of much importance, approaches.

The usher, having announced to the Basha our arrival at his
threshold, returned to show us the way. Proceeding through a
narrow passage, we arrived at the Meshwa, or seat of council.
This hall was divided into two compartments by a line of arches,
and the inner floor was raised three steps above the outer. Upon
this again there was a second elevation, which is considered the
place of honour, and here was seated his excellency. Near him
were placed two *chairs* for his Christian visitors. The usher,
having made a very low obeisance, retired.

The Cid Abd Selam E'Slowy gave us a cordial welcome,
shaking hands and pressing his own to his heart in token of his
friendly feeling. Our host, the consular agent, who stood bare-
footed at the entrance of the Meshwa, was saluted in his turn,
and then retired.

The Basha was reclining on a rich carpet, supported by round
velvet cushions embroidered in gold. Numerous letters lay

* The Great House.   I

around him, some open, others with the seal yet unbroken, and amongst the former I observed, placed upon a cushion exalted above the rest, a broad letter stamped on the top with the great seal of the Sultan. His excellency was dressed in a pale green caftan, over which was a fine muslin robe. He had wide trowsers of a light coloured yellow cloth; his girdle was of red leather, embroidered in silk, with silver clasp; he wore on his head the common Fez cap, circled by a white turban; and over all fell a transparent haik of the finest texture: in his hand he held a rosary. His manners were graceful and gentlemanly, and a pleasant smile gave an agreeable expression to his features. The father of this potentate was Basha over half the empire, and proved a good friend to the English during the war in the Peninsula, when we depended much on West Barbary for the supply of our armies, and also of our fleets in the neighbouring seas. It was Nelson's observation, that, should Great Britain be at war with any European maritime state, Marocco must be friendly to us, or else we must obtain possession of Tangier.

Abd Selam E'Slowy is, I believe, as good a man as his father; but he has not his capacity nor his energy of character.

After the usual compliments had passed, and I had explained the object of my journey, the Basha expressed his willingness to render me every assistance, adding, that if I would leave to him the choice, he would not rest till he had found a mare that " should make bright the face of all parties."

I did not accept the offer, as I had little faith in his knowledge of horse-flesh; and it occurred to me that, if I were hereafter to disapprove his selection, I might grievously and perhaps very inconveniently offend him. Declining therefore his proposition, on the ground of the trouble it would give him, I requested to be furnished with a letter to the Sheikh of Ibdowa, whose tribe was said to possess the finest breed of horses in the north of Marocco. He acceded to this request; and to give the letter the greater effect, directed that one of his attendants, " a kaid of a hundred," should accompany us.

As we were about to take our leave, he told me that he had been unwell for several days, and—as the people of his country invariably suppose that the Nazarene must be learned in medicine—he insisted upon my prescribing a suitable remedy. In vain I protested my ignorance of the healing art. He still persisted in his request; so I was forced, maugre my honesty, to undertake to play the doctor, and having promised to send him a dose, we parted the best of friends.

I remember, on one occasion, travelling in this country with a companion who possessed some knowledge of medicine: we had arrived at a dooar, near which we were about to pitch our tents, when a crowd of Arabs surrounded us, cursing and swearing at the "rebellers against God." My friend, who spoke a little Arabic, turning round to an elderly person, whose garb bespoke him a priest, said—"Who taught you that we are disbelievers? Hear my daily prayer, and judge for yourselves:" he then repeated the Lord's prayer. All stood amazed and silent, till the priest exclaimed—

"May God curse *me*, if ever I curse again those who hold such belief; nay, more, that prayer shall be my prayer till my hour be come. I pray thee, O Nazarene, repeat the prayer, that it may be remembered and written amongst us in letters of gold."

We then pitched our tents in peace, and shortly afterwards were visited by the priest, who, entering our tent with a sorrowful face, told us his child was sick in bed, and begged we would come and cure him. We went to the tent, and found the invalid in a burning fever. My friend prescribed some harmless medicine, which was immediately taken in our presence: an hour afterwards the boy was a corpse. A murmur ran through the village that the Nazarenes had poisoned the child: so ere the following morning dawned we had struck our tent and were hastening our departure, fearing the fanaticism of the inhabitants : but before we had time to depart, the father came to us bringing a bowl of milk. "Accept this, O Christians," he said, "in return for your kindly feeling towards my dear child; and think not that I join the ignorant in supposing you caused or wished his death. His hour had come; he is now happy; and God's will be done."

The inhabitants of Laraiche are ill-favoured, and very different from the generality of the Moorish race, who have fine features and athletic forms. There seems to be in this town a great mixture of the Negro with the native blood; and the countenance of every one you meet is marked with ill-health. There is much intermittent fever and ague prevalent in some seasons—occasioned probably by the quantity of flooded land and marshes in the neighbourhood.

This being the Jews' sabbath, we went with our host to the synagogue—a miserable room, wherein were assembled some twenty Hebrews, wretched in appearance, whose high-priest, a greasy-faced Rabbi, was standing before a dirty desk, and held in his hand a still dirtier book of prayers. Seated on wooden benches against the walls, these degenerate sons of Israel were moving their heads to and fro, like wild beasts in a cage, mumbling their orisons. Religion seemed to be with them a mere outward form, for they nodded to a friend or frowned at an enemy, even whilst chanting the sacred Psalms. One or two young men were called up by the Rabbi to read a chapter for the day from a large and beautifully written volume of the Bible. This they did in their usual sing-song voice, and as each returned to his seat his hand or robe was kissed by all he passed.

In front of a recess, wherein the sacred scrolls were deposited, was suspended a lamp, in the shape of a gigantic glass tumbler, held within a brazen frame-work formed to represent the seal of Solomon. The holy receptacle was now opened, and the hallowed roll of the Law and the Prophets exposed to the eyes of the congregation; after which it was carried in procession round the synagogue, and then replaced with religious care.

It is painful to look upon these degraded Israelites. Gross ignorance, bigotry, and depravity are stamped upon their features; and the hump of slavery rises markedly between their shoulders. Glad were we to get again into purer air.

The Don and I paid a visit to our nags, which were picketed within a battery overlooking the harbour. This is a spot which in general the Franks are forbidden to enter; as the Moors say they fear we might learn their art in gunnery: but the real reason, I suspect, is that they are ashamed we should perceive the misery of their mock defences, and their honeycombed guns mounted upon rotten carriages. I found, however, in the battery one handsome brass twelve-pounder, having an Arabic inscription. It appeared to be of Portuguese workmanship, and, I suppose, had been one of the trophies wrested by the Moors from their old invaders, who for so many ages domineered over the African Al Garb, whence their kings were styled " Rey de Portugal e de los Algarves."

In Tangier there is a cannon which, in consequence of its having been the means of destroying a vessel of the Christians which had entered the harbour with hostile intention, is said to be gifted with miraculous power. Pregnant women are often to be seen sitting on the gifted gun; their object being to be spared from the severer pains of childbirth.

Having obtained a guard from the governor, we proceeded to walk round Laraiche, and, entering a vineyard, were shown the Christians' burial-ground. A thicket of briers and rank weeds almost conceals the few monuments of the dead that remain unviolated; so we gave our consular agent a small sum, requesting he would cause the ground to be cleared and earthen mounds raised over the bodies of some poor sailors which had recently been interred in this melancholy spot.

The walls of the place are lofty, and in better preservation than those of most other towns in this region. The masonry of the Portuguese is that which is chiefly conspicuous, although no doubt the eye of an antiquary would discover traces of earlier lords of Laraiche than either the Portuguese or the Moors themselves. One feature in the fortifications of this old place struck us as peculiar : there is a salient angle on the land-front, of not more, I think, than ten degrees in width, but evidently adapted to the position with more skill in the art of defensive architecture than could have been expected at so early a period. We passed the outer market-place and the slaughter-ground, and then descending towards the river, had a view of the palace of the half-Irish Sultan Mulai Yezeed.

The following sketch of the history and character of this potentate was given me by an honest and intelligent native :—

In the middle of the last century, Seedy Mohamed was shaded by the Shereefian umbrella, or, as we should say, sat on the throne of Marocco. At that period the degenerate Moors still retained some remnant of their former glory, and of the learning handed down to them by the conquerors of Spain, their polished yet dreaded ancestors. Seedy Mohamed was a man of great energy, and endowed with a good capacity; but, being of a fanciful disposition, he prided himself, amongst other vagaries, on possessing in his harem a woman of every caste and clime.

At the commencement of his reign, in addition to other improvements which had been made throughout the empire, he was desirous to complete the defences of the wealthy city of Fas; and, knowing the superiority of the hated and despised Christian in engineering, he applied to the British government for the assistance of some person skilled in this art.

The request was acceded to, and an experienced sergeant of the corps of Sappers and Miners having been selected as a fit and sufficiently skilful person, he was placed at the disposition of his Imperial Majesty. Seedy Mohamed received the sergeant with much kindness, and allotted a suitable house for himself and his wife, a comely Irish lass, whom he had wedded a short time previous to leaving his native land. The sergeant, whose name is said to have been Brown, continued in the service of the Sultan several years after he had completed the required work at Fas, being well contented with the treatment he received from the Moorish potentate; but his course was run, and he died, leaving his widow childless.

After the usual shrieking and feasting by the disconsolate dame, at the wake of her late spouse, in which she was lustily accompanied by her Moorish acquaintances—who, indeed, rivalled by their howlings the best attended funeral in the land of Erin—she sought, with sorrowful heart, an interview of the Sultan, in order to beseech his majesty to grant her a pension and the means of returning to her own country. Seedy Mohamed was much struck by the appearance of the comely although red-haired young widow; he received her with benevolence, and at once granted her petition. But, before he dismissed her from his presence, he inquired whether she had a home, and if her parents were still alive. She said she was an orphan, and that she had few or no relations left who cared for her.

" God's pity on you," said the Sultan. " Why leavest thou this blessed land? Here you have friends and those who care for you. Become a true believer, and enter into that abode of unspeakable felicity, the Shereefian harem."

" God forbid," replied our countrywoman, " that either I should change my faith or become the concubine of any man."

Seedy Mohamed met this opposition with kingly offers and much kind persuasion ; and as he, who had never before heard a woman's refusal, was repulsed in his advances by a low-born and simple-minded Nazarene, the flame of love kindled with vast celerity in his royal breast.

" Keep thy faith, then, pretty Infidel," said the monarch. " Be my wife, and, if God please, thou alone shalt be the beloved in my harem."

To become a Sultana few would have resisted, and Seedy Mohamed, having divorced that one of his four wives who had found least favour in his sight, took his Christian spouse according to the usual rights of Islam.

The following year there were great rejoicings, for the Irish Sultana had been brought to bed of a red-haired prince, who was named Yezeed, but better known in the Moorish annals as the *Zaar*, or, as we might say, Rufus.

Mulai Yezeed soon showed by his disposition that he had inherited many of the qualities both of his father and his mother. He was of a violent temper; liberal, even lavish, to those who served him faithfully ; cruel, yet often performing acts of kindness and charity, and very fond of the British, whose cause he openly espoused on all occasions, and to such a degree, that it became a source of much displeasure to his Imperial Father. He, on the contrary, was especially adverse to our race, for he declared that they disgusted him with a tone of equality, and even with a pretence to superiority, which could not be brooked by the Protector of the Faith and the Sultan of Sultans. Seedy Mohamed moreover was very partial to the Spaniards, who at that time were our avowed enemies.

Mulai Yezeed, finding at length that the court of his father, who accused him of intriguing with the English government against his throne, was becoming too hot for him, determined to flee from it, and directed his steps northward towards the town of Tetuan, which at that time was the residence of the representatives of all the European powers. Wherever he passed in his flight, he gained by his liberality the good will of the inhabitants. Persecuted from sanctuary to sanctuary, despairing of obtaining his father's pardon, he was ultimately driven into open rebellion. Having at length taken refuge with several of his followers in a holy village situated on the lofty mountains of Beni Hassen, which form part of the lower range of the Atlas, the fugitive prince was not only received with much respect by the villagers, but they declared their willingness to protect him.

This soon reached the ears of the Sultan, who issued a proclamation declaring that his son Yezeed was a traitor and a rebel; that a powerful army would be despatched to "eat up" every district, every town and hamlet, that dared yield him any shelter; and that as it had been understood Mulai Yezeed had taken refuge among the inhabitants of Beni Hassen, a host invincible should proceed thither forthwith, and should burn the sanctuary, and put to the sword every man, woman, and child, if the traitorous Yezeed were allowed to remain there.

The dread mandate of the Sultan was soon spread throughout all Beni Hassen, and the affrighted inhabitants besought Mulai Yezeed to have pity on them and leave the district.

The prince promised to do so, and saying " God's will be done," ordered his followers to the stirrup; and mounting his beautiful steed, which was picketed nigh to the great saint's sepulchre, stuck his spurs into its flank: but the noble beast refused to move; caresses and blows were alike in vain. "Behold!" cried the prince to the crowd of villagers which had collected to witness his departure, "behold the decree of fate! O ye of little faith! Ye dread the threats of a man, but ye fear not the warning of God, or the anger of your saint and patron Mulai Abd Selam."

Upon this, the most ancient of the villagers stepped forward, and addressing the prince, said: " O favoured by God, and protected by our saint! We have sinned against him, and violated the laws of hospitality, which bind us to afford refuge to all who seek it, of whatever nation or religion, and by whomsoever they may be persecuted, even were he the Protector of the Faith itself, and the living sword of our religion. Remain with us, O Prince! and not a hair of thy beard shall be injured, so long as there breathes a man of Beni Hassen able to fight in the path of God."

These doings having been quickly reported at the court, a

large army was assembled, and the Sultan placed himself at their head. But, as his Majesty was proceeding from out of the city of Fas, the shaft of the Shereefian umbrella broke; the Sultan trembled and the troops were halted, for this omen was from God. That night the Sultan was taken ill, and a few days afterwards expired.

Yezeed was immediately proclaimed Sultan and Prince of all the true Believers. One of his first acts was to behead the late vizir of his father, who had favoured the Spaniards, and to order his hand to be nailed on the door of the Spanish Consulate at Tetuan. This outrage was the cause of a rupture between Spain and Marocco, which continued during Mulai Yezeed's reign; which, however, was only of two years' duration, for he ended a reckless career at the early age of forty-three.

The tribes of Tleeg and Kholot having broken out into rebellion, this prince accompanied the army which was sent to subdue them. On one occasion, when his troops and the rebel tribes were hotly engaged, he stationed himself on a commanding height, whence he might witness the affair. Observing his troops to waver under a charge of the rebels, and flying from the field, Mulai Yezeed, furious with rage at the dastardly behaviour of his soldiers, rushed down upon them with his bodyguard, driving them back upon the enemy, who were thus in their turn discomfited, the Sultan himself charging, heedless of danger, into the thickest of the mêlée.

This rebellion being quelled, frightful acts of tyranny and a massacre of both innocent and guilty followed. For their ruthless tyrant acted up to one of his favourite maxims—"This empire can never be governed unless a stream of human blood flow daily from the gate of my palace to the gate of the town."

It was Mulai Yezeed who gave permission to the troops, at a time when they were clamouring for arrears of pay, to plunder during twenty-four hours the Jews' quarter in Fas. The helpless Israelites were rifled of all they possessed; and it is a proverbial retort given to this day by the Jews to any Moor who asks money of them—"Were you not present at the pillage of the Jewry?"

To return to our own story. With much ostentation our guide pointed out to us on the road-side a wretched wheeled vehicle, ruder even in construction and form than a very ancient Egyptian cart which I saw shortly after its discovery on the banks of the Nile. This is the only wheeled carriage I have met with in all Marocco. It was drawn by oxen, and was employed for transporting cannon-shot from the shore.

When Prince Frederick of Hesse-Darmstadt arrived in 1839 at Tangier, whither he exiled himself for some months, his Highness brought with him two carriages, which looked like those of the time of our great-great-grandsires. Finding that the local authorities objected to his making use of a wheeled vehicle in the town, he wrote to the Sultan, offering to pave the main street of Tangier, if permitted to use his carriages. The Shereefian monarch graciously consented, on condition that the Prince's vehicles were deprived of their wheels, as without that precaution the Protector of the Faithful feared that the lives of his loyal subjects would be exposed to imminent danger.

Strange to say, the Prince followed this injunction to the very letter, and one of his carriages, deprived of its wheels, was borne as a litter between two stout mules.

Such is the policy of the tyrant of West Barbary, who thinks that on this subject, as on all others, "ignorance is bliss," and who knows full well that the reforms, however imperfect, of his co-religionists in the Levant are already dragging rapidly to ruin the whole religious and political system of their false prophet. Not unreasonably then does the Moorish potentate conceive, like the Chinese, that his safest course is to avert the monster innovation, and to trust to the jealousy of Christian powers, and to *Een-Shaallah*,* for the endurance of his empire. But whether reform be admitted or not in a system now obsolete and unsustainable, one thing at least is certain—that the sword of empire falling, as it has been falling for several ages, from the grasp of the Moslem, the extinction of Mohamedanism throughout the world becomes every day more certain. And herein we find a striking fulfilment of our Saviour's prophetic declaration, " All they that take the sword shall perish with the sword."†

Early the following morning the bearer of the promised letter to the Sheikh of Ibdowa presented himself. He was a kaid, and

---

* If it please God.   † Matthew xxvi. 52.

a favourite attendant of the Basha. He was handsomely dressed, well mounted, and armed with the long gun and awkward Moorish sword, and on his saddle was a handsome carpet, together with saddle-bags containing pickets and barley for his horse. He brought also a loaf of bread for himself, and a small leathern bottle with a long cord to draw water from the wells. He had lately returned from the rebel provinces, which the Sultan had been "eating up," as the Moors term the proceedings of their rulers to punish rebellion. This process of "eating up" is carried into effect by the potentate's establishing a camp of some thousand men, principally cavalry, in the district of the rebels. The troops destroy in the most wanton manner what they and their horses may not require for sustenance, plunder the inhabitants of their goods and cattle, and, carrying off their women, leave the land completely desolate, and as bare of its fruits as if an army of locusts had overrun it.

During one of the late rebellions, a beautiful young girl was offered up as a propitiatory sacrifice, her throat being cut before the tent of the Sultan, and in his presence! Such sacrifices are now, happily, very rare, even in this benighted land; but oxen and horses are still frequently immolated, by penitent or over-awed rebels, to appease the offended potentate.

As we recrossed the river Al Kous, I inquired of our new companion how the Sultan manages to pass a river with his army. The kaid told me that either a bridge of rushes and reeds was made for the purpose, or, if these were wanting, the skins of animals were blown up, and covered with sticks and earth, over which the army marches; this enlightened race not having as yet arrived at so high a point of science as to be able to string together a dozen pontons.

CHAPTER XI.

Shemmees—Curious Remains—A Narrow Escape—Moorish Superstition—
Sadeed and Lokareesy—Feat of Alee—Prayers for Rain—Market of
Raisàna—Curious species of Barter—The Pass of the Camel's Neck—Ain
el Khader—Dinner with the Sheikh—Dispute about Pork—Arab Intrigue
—Sanctuary of Mulai Abd Selam—The Leaping-stone—Peculiar Rites
—The Graven Images—Curious Ruins at Tagsher—Story of the Ancient
Vase.

HAVING followed the course of the river for three miles, our
route took a southerly direction, and we halted to breakfast
under the shade of a wide-spreading fig-tree ; near to which was
a well, built of large hewn stones, apparently of great antiquity,
while around it were scattered the ruins of a building that had
evidently been of some importance. The kaid told us, that on
the top of the hill, at the foot of which we were then halting,
were the remains of an old city of the Room, called Shemmees ;
but that it was now avoided by man as the habitation of evil
spirits.

This information excited our curiosity, and Don José and
myself determined to visit the abode of Jins. So taking my
gun, as if in search of game, for I was well aware that our Laraiche guard, the kaid, would oppose a visit to the ancient town,
and accompanied by the Hadj, we left the kaid and the rest of
our party to discuss at their leisure a breakfast of bread and
water-melons ; and set out on what they would all have considered an enterprise as impious as it was perilous.

We toiled up the steep bank, and entered a narrow path
through thick brushwood ; the first object that presented itself
was a wall of solid masonry of large hewn stones, blackened
either by fire or by some other means which we could not divine.
The ground over which we passed sounded hollow under our
feet ; and the bushes became thicker and loftier as we advanced,
so that we were frequently obliged to creep on our hands and
knees in order to penetrate the jungle.

After considerable toil we come to a long line of wall, some thirty feet high, running apparently to the bottom of the south-eastern side of the hill. Having clambered through a hole in this wall, a large vault presented itself, extending some forty feet under ground; it was sixteen feet wide, and twenty in height; and near to it were several other vaults of smaller dimensions. Again we advanced through the thicket. The heat was intense, and my companion almost fainted from thirst; whilst the briers so intercepted our path, that had it not been for my compass, we should have been lost in the dense mass of vegetation.

We now came upon another lofty line of wall, where we observed very large hewn stones, and several truncated marble columns imbedded in the masonry; proving that the buildings, of which these walls were the ruins, had been constructed out of the materials of some beautiful edifice of yet higher antiquity.

We crept along the base of this wall, till we again got into more open ground; and, as I passed beneath a wild olive-tree, some large animal darted at me from one of the branches, grazing the collar of my coat, and then escaping into the bushes. I fancied it was a serpent, but the movement was so sudden, I could not distinguish its form.

We returned to the well, where I found the kaid much out of humour at our long absence. On relating our adventures, and mentioning the animal that had darted at me from the tree, Mallem Hamed exclaimed, " O fortunate Nazarene! the kaid was just telling us, that of those who have visited Shemmees few have returned; and that the evil spirits are sure to take the form of an alluring damsel, and draw their victims to destruction, or else, in the shape of a snake, or some wild animal, tear them to pieces." The kaid, with an air of grave displeasure, confirmed this account, and added that last year a young shepherd, whilst tending a flock at the foot of the hill, was darted at by a serpent from a tree, which bit him severely in the neck; and that the lad died before he reached his home.

When the mid-day heat moderated, we resumed our journey, and passed through the villages of Sadeed and Lokareesy. At four P.M. we entered the wood of Sahel, at a point about twelve miles to the southward of the road by which we had approached Laraiche. Here we crossed a beautiful rivulet, called *Boos-*

affee, or the Father of Clearness, and thence passed through
a large marsh, where the tracks and rootings of wild boar
abounded.   This spot, our guide informed us, had been the
scene of a feat of the Six-fingered while hunting the boar.

"Alee," he said, " had shot at and struck a large boar; the
wounded animal rushed at his assailant, who with one blow cut
the ferocious beast in two at the small of the back.   When the
hunters came up, some of them expressed their doubts as to the
possibility of the animal having been divided at one blow; on
which Alee drew his sword, which is described as having been
full five feet long, and grasping it with both hands, made a cut
into the stem of a cork-tree.   Then turning to the hunters, he
defied the strongest man amongst them to wrench the sword from
the tree: several attempts were made, but without success.
That very sword is now used by a fisherman of the Sebboo for
spearing *Shebbel,"* a very fine fish of the salmon genus, but white-
fleshed, which the Spaniards call *Sabalo,* being a corruption of
the Arabic name.   This fish is found in the Guadalquivir (the
Wad-al-Kibeer of Andalusia), and abounds in the Kous, and
several other rivers on the western coast of Marocco.

At five we sallied forth from the wood, and passed through a
large village called Leblet.   The inhabitants rushed out from
their houses to have a sight of the Ensara.

The country around was cultivated with the grain called drà,
and there was every prospect of a favourable harvest.   " God
be praised," said the kaid, " for his bounty: last year, in truth,
we had a sad prospect for the crops, and had not my master,
Seedy Abd Selam E'Slowy, ordered the Jews—God curse them!
—to pray for rain, I know not what would have become of God's
creatures! "

"Why did not the Mussulmen," said I, " offer up their
prayers? "

"So they did," he replied, " and for twenty days and nights,
—and to the banner of each mosque was affixed a prayer written
by the Fekee himself.   The prayers floated in the face of heaven
—but all in vain, for the prayers of the Faithful are like music
to God, who is worthy of all praise; and therefore the Almighty,
rejoicing in the sweet sound of our supplication, granteth not
the desires of our prayers, for he wishes us to continue still to

pray. But no sooner is he tormented with the disgusting prayers of Jews and infidels than he granteth forthwith their petitions, in order to be freed from their importunities." *

About six P.M. we arrived at the market-place of Raisàna, in which grew a fine tall palm-tree, an object of considerable rarity in the south of Algarb. On this spot are held on stated days in the year the markets, or, to speak more correctly, the fairs, at which the people assemble in large numbers to barter their merchandise and cattle, and the peculiarities of Moorish habits are never more strikingly displayed than on these occasions.

In the district of Bemin Sooar, a mountainous country inhabited entirely by Berber tribes, there is one place where, during the fair, a barter of a very curious kind takes place. This fair is held only once a year, and is chiefly resorted to for the purpose of bachelors finding wives, married men adding to their matrimonial treasures, and maidens or widows getting husbands. In fact, the whole affair resolves itself into the women selling themselves: but to escape the ignominy of such a procedure, the traffic is carried on in the following manner:

Each lady desiring to enter into wedlock dresses herself in her best and most becoming attire, and taking with her a piece of cloth of her own weaving, sits down unveiled in the market-place. The men, both young and old, who are candidates for matrimony, parade about the market examining the texture of the cloth displayed by the ladies, and scrutinizing at the same time their looks and behaviour. Should the customer be pleased with the maiden, he inquires the price of the cloth; she replies by naming what she would expect as a dowry, and the amount of this she raises or depresses according as the candidate for her heart may please her, resorting to the demand of an exorbitant sum should she be averse to the purchaser. During this barter, the enamoured swain is able, in some degree, to judge of her temper and character. If they come to an agreement, the parents of the girl are appealed to; and they have the right to assent or not, as they please. Should they assent, the parties adjourn to a public notary, the contract is made, and the purchased bride is carried off to her new home.

* Absurd as this may appear, it is, nevertheless, the general belief in Marocco.

In this traffic, widows are at a low price in general, and divorced ladies sell their cloths very cheap. The wife thus purchased cannot be resold, however much the purchaser may repent of his bargain. She is his *lawful wedded wife*, and retains the purchase money, which is her jointure or dowry.

It is evident that this curious system of barter has been resorted to by these Mahomedan mountaineers as a means of evading the law of the Prophet, which interdicts all courtship before marriage.

After leaving the market-place and its beautiful palm-tree, a wide extent of plain lay before us, and the curling smoke that rose from various spots marked the position of Arab encampments.

Having crossed the plain, we entered a pass called the *Camel's Neck*. Here we sprung a large flock of the small bustard, called by the Moors *Boozarat;* they are of excellent flavour, and about the size of our black-cock.

At sunset we reached Ain el Khàder, or the Green Fountain, the site of an encampment of the tribe of Ibdor. At this spot we pitched our tent, and were visited by a son of the sheikh, who, on the part of his father, invited us to dinner, which, he said, was all prepared and waiting for us.

We accepted the invitation, and found our host within his tent, seated on a cushion covered with the skin of a Caracal lynx, which is said to possess one property of inestimable value in this country, to wit, that a flea will never settle on it; and close to this, fine sheep-skins had been placed for his guests.

"Welcome, welcome," said the sheikh; and when we were seated he added, "Are your seats comfortable? Have you all you require? Are you satisfied?"

I replied by pouring out a redundancy of blessings on him and all his family and race, especially his great-great-grandfather.

All further conversation was cut short by one of his slaves, Abd el Habeeb, appearing with a Moorish table, beautifully carved and painted in Arabesque. It was of a circular form, about two feet in diameter, and raised some six inches from the ground, which, squatting as we were around it, was a very convenient elevation.

Upon this table was placed a large Moorish bowl containing

a thick soup, with some kind of vermicelli in it, and highly seasoned with red peppers. In the savoury mess were four wooden spoons of grotesque form, with which we set to work most heartily. The next dish was a stew of beef, accompanied with slices of melon to sharpen the appetite; and then appeared the usual conical dish of kesksoo. During the repast not a word was spoken, except it were the ejaculations of *Bismillah* (in the name of God), *al Handoo-billah* (thanks to God), or perhaps a *Saffee Allah* (may God pardon me).

At length the Don and I were compelled to give up the attack upon the mountain of kesksoo, to the evident sorrow and surprise of the sheikh, who, as well as the kaid, continued for a long time to assault it vigorously.

The ample dish being at last removed, the sheikh broke silence by saying, "Truly, you *Christians* have made but a poor feast. You require pig—that is your proper food, I am told; and without it you do not thrive. They tell me too," he added, "that you milk your pigs : wonderful indeed it is how the Lord's creatures err ! "

"Blessings upon your beard ! " said I : "what false ideas you Moslems have regarding the followers of Seedna Aisa !* But let me talk with you about this meat of pig."

"God forbid ! " said the Arab; " it is a sin even to think of it."

"Sin to think of pig ? " said I, taking him up rather quickly : "Sin, do you call it? Tell me, O follower of the Prophet, who made the pig ? "

"God," replied the sheikh.

"Then," said I, "according to your account, God created sin."

The old sheikh reflected for a moment, and turning to the Mallem, said—

"Of a truth, the young Nazarene has entrapped me; I never heard it put in that way before. But, O Christian, why should the prophet of God—blessed be his name!—have forbidden us to eat thereof?"

"I will endeavour to enlighten your mind," said I; "and, if it please God, you shall understand.

* The Lord Jesus.

K

" Know, then, O sheikh, that the flesh of the pig is unwhole-
some food in a hot country ; and a heavy fine is imposed on who-
soever kills a pig during the hot months, even in the Christian
lands of Spain and Italy : in the hotter climes of India it is
rarely eaten, either by Christian or pagan.   The prophet Moses,
and your prophet also, who, on this subject, adopted the precept
of the great Jewish legislator, forbade it to their followers ; but
the Messiah, blessed for ever, the Lord Jesus of Nazareth, gave
us, his disciples, thence called Nazarenes, that divine law which
was designed from the beginning to supersede the formalities of
the Mosaic dispensation, and he taught us, in his far more enlightened code, that ' there is nothing unclean in itself.' * Seedna
Aisa by his heavenly wisdom foresaw that his followers would
be wise in their generation, and would avoid excess."

The old sheikh listened with great attention to this long ora-
tion, which I uttered with the gravity of tone that so serious a
theme demanded ; and when I paused he remained some time
silent, as if pondering my words.

Although I knew too much of the Arab character to expect
to make him a convert, I could not refrain from going on.

" Some six hundred years," I said, " before your lawgiver,
Mohamed of Mecca, flourished, Seedna Aisa, the Messiah, appeared on earth and gave us forth those laws by which we have
since been governed.   The goodness of them is to be estimated
by the prosperity of Christendom, at least of all those regions of
it wherein the Divine will has not been thwarted by the evil
machinations and superstitious schemes of some of his pretended
followers, who take the name of Christian, but do not make the
Gospel of Christ their rule.   Christ has allowed us to eat pork ;
but he has commanded us not to bear false witness against our
neighbour ; he has said, ' Thou shalt not lie.'   See, in yonder
town, which we left yesterday, no Jew or Moslem would taste
of pig ; but few are there, I fear, that for the gain of a few
moozoonats † would not give false evidence.   They can be strict
followers of the law in what is unimportant, but they are breakers
of it in what is of great moment.   Pardon me, O sheikh, but
you know the truth of what I assert."

* Rom. xiv. 14.
† A moozoonat is composed of six floos, equal to about a penny sterling.

" Very curious," replied he, " and you have spoken much truth : " and upon this he fell into a brown study. I had not, however, any great idea that I had made a convert, and indeed if I had, his next words would have dispelled the illusion. For, still harping upon the ' father of tusks,' he said, almost with a sigh, " I am told that there is only one part of the pig which is forbidden ; but, unluckily, our prophet forgot to mention which. May God have mercy on us all ! "

" Amen," I responded ; and we changed the conversation.

It was a fine moonlight night as we returned to our quarters, and all was silent, except now and then the distant howling of the jackal. The Hadj challenged us, as we neared the tent, with the single word "allee ? " (who ?).

" God be blessed," cried I, " for good men who watch and pray preparing for the world to come."

" *May your end be happy*," * replied the Hadj ; and we all betook ourselves to rest.

In the night we were awakened by a loud screaming, the cause of which was an amorous young Arab, who had entered by stealth the tent of his sweetheart, with whom he had arranged a rendezvous, the father being absent at Laraiche. The mother was supposed by the lovers to be asleep, but she had only been dosing, and even in that state of semi-repose she had kept one eye open. The matron, supposing the young man was a thief, screamed for help, in which the girl, treacherous to her lover, deemed it prudent to join, declaring that all the young man said about an assignation was false, and so well did she play her part that the sheikh ordered the culprit to be secured, and gave directions that he should be sent the next day to prison at Laraiche, to be judged by the law of the Prophet.

Before six in the morning we were on horseback ; the Arabs were in a state of much commotion, for the amorous swain had escaped in the night, and was supposed to have taken the road to the sanctuary of Mulai Abd Selam, and it was well known that it would require an extraordinary mandate from the Sultan to violate that great sanctuary, in order to arrest a criminal charged with even deeper offences than this man.

---

* This expression, when used by a Mohamedan, signifies a hope that you may be converted to Islamism before death.

The sanctuary of Mulai Abd Selam is situated on the rugged Sierra of Beni Hassen, whose snow-capped heads are seen from the Straits of Gibraltar towering above the lesser hills around the city of Tetuan. Here all that was mortal of that inspired person—one who, in the "land of the infidel Nazarenes, who rebel against God, would have been profanely called a madman" —is deposited, and, like the holy Kaaba, Mulai Abd Selam has usurped the site where his ancestors worshipped before their eyes were opened to the knowledge of the one only God.

Early in the spring of every year, pilgrims visit the holy shrine, and I gathered the following account of their journey from Hadj Hamed Asharky, brother of my servant, who was himself a seven-fold pilgrim, and whose mother could boast of having knelt at the sepulchre of the saint on seventeen different occasions.

A kaffla of some hundred souls having been collected, composed of men, women, and children, mounted on beasts of burden of every degree, from the gigantic camels to diminutive donkeys, and each family being provided with a little tent, they are marched in triumphal procession through the streets of Tangier, with flags flying, and the *ghaita* and *tebel* (the pipes and drum) joining in horrid discord.

They pass the first night at the village of Mahoga, a short distance south of Tangier. The next day they proceed through an extensive undulating plain ; and then, having passed a rugged line of hills, encamp at the foot of Beni Hassen. About noon the following day, they are blessed with the view of the white-washed tomb of Seedy Abd Selam, overhung by the rock of the "Sakht el Waladeen," or "the mother's wrath and judgment." Here again they pitch their tents, for at this spot a ceremony must be performed.

A flat white stone of circular form, smooth as if polished by man, and of a substance like marble, is the object of religious veneration. It is called the Leaping-stone, and such of the pilgrims as can jump over it are looked upon as blessed by the Deity ; whereas the evil-disposed are sure, when they make the attempt, either to alight on the stone or to touch some part of it. It is raised but a few inches from the ground, and appears so small, that the Hadj fancied he could almost stride it. He said, however, that he had never attempted to leap over it; for amongst hundreds whom he had witnessed make the trial, there were not half a dozen who succeeded: " and this," said he, with a look of sadness, " is a melancholy proof of the wickedness of man in these degenerate days."

The next morning the kaffla proceeds, passing the house where Mulai Yezeed dwelt, when he sought refuge in this sanctuary from the vengeance of his father the Sultan Mohamed. Then the train ascends the holy mount of Mulai Abd Selam; and so steep is the ascent, that women and children are obliged to dis-mount, wending their way through a wood of wild olive and other forest trees, every one of which is leaning in act of adoration towards the holy site. On this mount the air is cool even in the hottest months; and every pilgrim's heart throbs with anxiety as he approaches the holy ground.

No sooner do they come within the confines of the village, than they are beset by numerous children of the Shereefian inhabitants, descendants of the saint, and guardians of their ancestor's venerated shrine. Small sweet biscuits have been provided as an offering to these holy urchins, and while they scramble for these the kaffla is allowed to proceed without further molestation.

They now enter the village, which is composed of thatched huts, and here again they pitch their tents. At night the camp is visited by the Shereefs, to each of whom a small gift is presented according to the means of the donor; but here, as in various other countries, the old adage is found too true, that the greater the saint the greater the rogue; for the pilgrims are obliged to keep a sharp watch all night, as petty pilfering seems to be one of the most distinguishing characteristics of the descendants of Mulai Abd Selam.

Next morning they rise with the dawn, and go in procession, accompanied by the Shereefs, to the Mkadem, or chief of the sanctuary, to whom also an offering is to be made. They are then allowed to pass on; and, ascending the mountain by steps hewn in the rock, are conducted to the mouth of a cave, of which the entrance is so low that even children are obliged to crawl on their hands and knees. At length they come to a vast cavity with a lofty vault. Into this the guides do not allow the pilgrims to penetrate.

Here are pointed out to the Faithful the "*graven images*," as they are called. These consist of the figure of a snake half coiled and with its neck erect, having before it the figures of a man and a woman, naked and in a squatting position, one of whom holds in its hand what is said to be a drum, or, according to Hadj Hamed, a sphere. This carved work is about five feet from the ground, and is in high relief.

The Shereefs, after having taken due care to impress upon the minds of the pilgrims that these petrified personages are kept in a charmed state by the power of the sainted Abd Selam, the procession again moves on, and reaches next the famous rock of the *Sakht el Waladeen*, or "the mother's curse."

This is a narrow fissure in the rock, extending perpendicularly down to a pit which, as the people assert, is bottomless; a ledge of a few inches in breadth has been cut on one border of the fissure, as a footing for those courageous pilgrims who attempt to pass through it.

The bold votary who resolves to make the fearful trial, presses his back against the side of the rock, opposite to that on which the ledge is cut, upon which ledge he fixes his feet, and thus advances, with the greatest caution, sideways. During all this time the pilgrim has his body suspended over the dark gulf. Near the extremity of the fissure, he arrives at the point of greatest difficulty; for there the sides of the cleft approach so near each other, that to squeeze through is scarcely possible. If he pass through the extremity of the fissure, the pilgrim obtains, as a special blessing, that his heart shall bear no evil will towards his parents. But should the attempt be made by the wicked, the rock closes; and the sinner is held prisoner, until the Shereefs, repeating some mystic verses and praying to Allah, the chasm yawns, and the pilgrim is enabled to retrace his steps to the point from whence he set out.

Hadj Hamed declares that, fat or thin, it makes no difference, and that a very thin man, who may have even stripped himself to the waist to reduce his bulk, may often be seen held fast, as he tries to force his way through the narrow opening while a

fat man, with all his clothes on, shall pass through with ease.
"This," he added, "all depends upon God, and the power dele-
gated to the saint, who knows men's hearts." Hadj Hamed said
further, that he never had any difficulty himself in passing. I
must remark, however, that the Hadj is very spare in form, and
not incommoded with a superabundance of raiment.

The pilgrims, on their return homeward, pray at the shrine
of Mulai Abd Selam; and next day make the best of their way
to Tangier.

But to return to our own pilgrimage.

As we departed from the Ibdor encampment, we observed
troops of boys and girls employed in scaring away the doves,
which commit great havoc among the corn in this region. Some
of the boys showed themselves most dexterous slingers.

In about half an hour we passed a small building on the top
of a mount, being the tomb of Seeyed Yamani. Some six miles
south of us stood a conical hill, called Tagsher; near which, as
I learned from the kaid, are some curious ruins. He described
them as being those of a large castle, built of extraordinary
materials, every stone being of such a size that no hundred men
of modern times could move it: some of them, he said, were as
much as twenty feet square and about fifteen feet high.

He described the entrances as having been blocked up by
earth and sand, except in one place through which he had
entered and proceeded some distance under ground; the passage
becoming at last so narrow that he could not advance further,
although by the light he perceived it was of yet greater extent.
At a short distance from the building lay a flat stone, which he
lifted up, and found beneath it a pit, that, by his description,
was of an inverted conical form: it was empty.

The kaid said, that in a part of the road over which we were
travelling there are remains of an underground aqueduct: and
last year there were found in a well, a brazen horse, small
brazen men—as he called them—and some lamps, also of the
same metal. Unfortunately all these things had been broken to
pieces by those who found them, and sold in secret to Jew pedlars as old brass.

The difficulty experienced in obtaining any valuable relics of
the various nations that have conquered and colonized this

country is mainly to be attributed to the well known rapacity of
the government; which, according to the law, has the right of
seizing all treasure or other objects of value that may be discovered: and most barbarous acts of cruelty are often exercised,
in extorting confessions from such unfortunate individuals as
may be accused of having discovered any such.

The following instance of this was related to me as a well
known fact :—

Some years ago, when Alarby E'Saidy was governor of Tangier, and dealt out his justice by weight of gold and silver, one
Mohamed, a poor countryman, who dwelt a few miles distant
from tne ancient city of Booammar, around which lie scattered
many old ruins, was ploughing a slip of land which had evidently lain fallow for many years: the land had lately been
given to him as a reward for two years' hard service in active
warfare, under the banners of his sultan, against the rebel tribe
Oodaia: a method not unusual of recompensing the militia,
who constitute the armed force of this empire. In an adjoining field was a fellow-villager actively employed in the same
pursuit.

Now Mohamed's ploughshare happened to strike against some
obstacle; which, on examination, proved to be a large earthen
vase of curious form. Mohamed, finding it sound, and thinking
it might be of service to his family for fetching water from the
village well, went to the border of the field, where he had left
his outer garments, and there deposited it.

The discovery, and honest Mohamed's subsequent movements,
were not unobserved by his neighbour; who suspected from his
silence that there was more found than an earthen pot. So, on
returning from his day's labour, he told the village gossips that
Mohamed had assuredly found a treasure; for he had marked
him, whilst ploughing, turn up a large pot, which appeared to
be very heavy, and which he had immediately hidden under his
clothes, and had not said one word to him about it, although he
was hard by.

The following was a market-day, when the villagers of
Booammar flocked as usual to Tangier. The news of Mohamed's discovery was soon spread among the town's-folk, and
it was not long ere it reached the soldiers, the alert spies of old

Alarby E'Saidy; to whom they quickly reported the tale, with no few exaggerations.

Mohamed, unsuspicious of impending evil, was disposing of his little produce, when the rude hands of two soldiers arrested him; and, as is usual in this country, without any reason given, dragged him before the grey-bearded Hakem.

" So, I have caught you at last, you rascal. You have found a treasure and not reported it. Speak, and let us know the amount: and look to your words."

Mohamed told his story, which was a plain one; and, begging for mercy, requested, in order to prove the truth of his statement, that a soldier might be sent to search his house and bring the pot, which would be delivered up by his family. The kaid agreed, and Mohamed was, in the mean time, confined in prison.

The soldier made the search, and nothing was found but the empty vase. On this being announced to the Kaid Alarby, Mohamed was again brought before him.

" I am not," said the ruthless magistrate, "to be imposed upon by such small cunning. Down with him, let him have five hundred stripes, and then see if he will declare his hiding-corner for his ill-gotten wealth."

To hear was to obey: and the unfortunate ploughman received full five hundred blows from the dreaded whip of Tsafilelts; but he persisted to the last lash in saying that he had found no treasure.

" Back with him to the dungeon," said the kaid: and the wretched Mohamed was carried half senseless to prison.

A month passed; and every day his poor wife trudged to town with his scanty meal: for Moorish authorities rarely bestow a morsel of food on their prisoners, leaving them to depend solely upon what may be brought by their families, who are not prevented giving the prisoners every kind of luxury, if they be able to afford it.

The little property Mohamed possessed was soon exhausted. His wife had a young family, and having no means of supporting both them and her husband, extreme want soon stared her in the face. Exhaustion of body and anguish of mind brought on a violent fever, which confined her to the hut.

Thus day after day passed away; no one brought Mohamed his usual pittance, and no one came to soothe him in his misery: so that, had it not been for the charity of some fellow-prisoners, the honest ploughman must have died of starvation. The jailer, however, was more humane than most of his trade; and, seeing the truly wretched state of his prisoner, endeavoured to intercede in his behalf with Kaid Alarby, but the tyrant was inflexible "Let God be witness," said he, "I never will free him till he give up the treasure."

Upon being informed of this, poor Mohamed fell on the ground, tore his beard, and swearing by God and his prophet, cried out, " There is no justice on earth; our religion and our law are all void! But hark ye," said he to the jailer, "tell the governor that I submit to his will, and he shall have the treasure: tell him to send with me guards, and I will deliver up my riches." Mohamed's eye looked wild as he spoke, and the jailer knew not whether he was frantic or in his right mind.

" Aha!" said the kaid, upon hearing of his having confessed; "I knew we should bring him to his senses. Send with him a couple of stout fellows; and let them be on the look-out, that he does not conceal any part of his wealth."

Mohamed was conducted with shackles on his legs to Booammar. As he entered the village he learnt that his poor wife had died of sickness and grief, and that his children were supported by the miserable tell-tale, who had since bitterly repented of the injury he had thoughtlessly done to his honest neighbour, and had even offered the kaid a handsome present to induce him to free poor Mohamed from thraldom.

On reaching the ploughman's dwelling, the soldiers were about to enter with him: "Stop," said he, "every man's house is sacred; wait a little, and I will show you all."

The soldiers would have disregarded Mohamed's request; but a murmur of indignation ran through the crowd of villagers at such disregard of their customs.

A few minutes elapsed, when Mohamed again appeared at his threshold: but now he had his gun with him; and two little children were clinging to their father's knees, calling for notice from their long-absent parent.

The soldiers fell back, thinking he intended violence to them;

but this was far from the poor man's thoughts. He had attached a string to the trigger of his gun, and passing it behind
the stock, now put the muzzle to his head. The soldiers, perceiving his object, were rushing forward to seize him, when he
cried out, " Tell the kaid that this alone remains for me to
give—my blood. Let it be on his head!" and pulling the
string, he fell a corpse.

The soldiers returned, and reported what had happened.
" Awa?" (Is that all?) said the kaid; " so he lied after all:
God have mercy upon his soul!" And thus was wound up the
affair of the ancient vase.

CHAPTER XII.

Cross the river Ayasha—Tribe of Ibdowa—Moorish Letter—The Hara of Ibdowa—Cause of Degeneracy—Tortures—English turned Bedouins—Sheikh's Story—The British Sultan—Had-el-Gharbeea—Ancient Well—Tame Tortoises—Arab Ladies.

EARLY in the morning we crossed the river Ayasha, running north and south. The soil of the country around is particularly rich, though its surface is covered with flints.

At nine o'clock we came in sight of the thatched dwelling of the sheikh of the tribe of Ibdowa, situated on a rising ground above an Arab encampment. It was to this sheikh that the letter of the basha was addressed, desiring him to afford me every assistance in purchasing a mare of the finest breed.

As we approached the dwelling, I perceived the Arab chief. He was an elderly man, dressed in a handsome cloth kaftan, with a haik of the purest white; and was seated under the shade of the thatched roof, which projected some feet from the walls. I remained mounted at a short distance whilst the kaid of our party advanced, and, after respectfully saluting the chief, drew from his bosom the basha's letter, kissed it, and handed it to him.

The sheikh, having examined the seal, bestowed on it a hearty smack, and lifted the letter to his forehead. As he read the contents, he took one or two scrutinizing looks at my Nazarene ship, and then remained wrapped for some moments in thought, as if wondering whether any other interpretation could be put upon the basha's recommendation to afford a Christian assistance in the purchase of a horse; in short, whether some deep matters of national importance were not concealed under a surface of horse-dealing.

What the exact import of this epistle was, I do not know: but as it may be interesting to the reader to have a specimen of a Moorish letter, I give the following translation of one which

I received from an important person among the saints, who are the hereditary nobility of this country :—

"Praise to the One God !

The blessings of God Almighty on our Lord Mahomed, and upon his friends and followers be peace !

"Praise be to God that sent his prophets as mediators between Him and His creatures, who redeemed his servants from the shades of ignorance and brought them to the light of the path of righteousness through the grace of God, who alone is worthy of all honour. No one on earth is like unto Him; He gives not account of aught that He works; mankind must render their account hereafter to Him; He has sealed the missions of the prophets by the most excellent lord in the creation—Mahomed—the exalted above all. May God bless him, his followers, and friends, who are the most excellent among the nations, and ancient above all ! Peace be upon him that followeth the true path and that submits himself to God's will."

Which premised :—

"From the most excellent Shereef of most noble ancestry, descended from a most renowned stock, son of our Lord Gelool, grandson of the great blessing unto mankind our Lord Aly Ben Gelool Alkadeery Al Hasàny, great-grandson of the Holy, the brilliant pole of the universe, renowned in all regions for his powerful protection to all that were afflicted or distressed by sea or by land, the Sheikh Mulai Aly Alkadeery.

"We address one who is our friend and skilled both in the management of the pen and of the sword, and excelling in soundness of mind. We bless you from the depth of our heart; and we pray that God protect and behold you, preserving you from all evil, and may God make you to see the true religion and take away all enemies, that hereafter heaven may be your residence.

"If you inquire concerning us, we are in good health, and in happiness so long as you may enjoy it likewise,—thank God ! We pray Him that we may soon meet; and He is prompt in answering our prayers.

"Know, O beloved Nazarene ! that I have made acquaintance

with an intelligent Faquee, a learned astronomer, a timekeeper and professor of the sciences; his name is Seedy Mohamed Ben al Fadal Esoosy. I have examined and found such character in him as shall be esteemed and approved of by you for knowledge of the arts and sciences; and he has entreated me to present him to you.

"He shall, if it please God, be the means of your obtaining the large work of Ibn Batoota,* which exists in the Shereefian library of Wazàn; for the shereefs of that city esteem Seedy Esoosy as the pupil of their eye.

"I beg you to be kind to him; and, above all, not to overlook his thirst for knowledge; and may God, worthy of all praise and honour, inspire you with his wisdom.

"Do not suppose that I am forgetful about the horse. By the living God, I have not found what will suit you; but, *Eenshaallah*, your mind shall be set at rest. Write to us without fail! without fail! Peace!

"17th Jooniad, the first year, 1252 (September, 1836)."

When I supposed that the old sheikh had concluded his deliberations, I dismounted, and approached him with a due proportion of saláms. He rose to meet me, saying, "Welcome, O Nazarene! On my head be it to serve you, both in observance of my lord the Basha's orders, and because the English are known by us to be honourable men and friends to the Emsulmeen. But, young man," added the sheikh, "I fear you will not find in all this district a suitable animal."

"Where shall I seek a horse then, O my best of friends," I inquired, "if it be not in Ibdowa?"

"Listen," said he, "and understand. A few years past my tribe boasted of the finest bone and blood in the country. The care of a Bedouin towards his mare was like that of a mother towards her child; never was it allowed to quit his sight, and if he heard of a famous stallion, were it on the confines of the deserts of Soos, he would travel in the season, and pay any sum to have a good cross for the mare he gloried in. When in foal,

---

* This rare work of the ancient African geographer I subsequently obtained through the good offices of the 'learned timekeeper and professor of sciences.' A careful transcript of it was shortly afterwards presented by me to the Royal Asiatic Society in London.

no horse of bad form or below the standard height was allowed
to pass within view of the hara.   But, as with all mortals, our
day of sorrow has come, and the wreck of our former pride is
yet to be witnessed among some sorry mares, which I will point
out in yonder field; now from age and neglect unworthy your
purchase.   Look," said he, "at their degraded offspring, those
colts which my slave is driving; look at their form and size,
they are mere pack animals."

"This is strange," I observed: "whence this neglect of your
own interests?"

The old horse-breeder looked at our kaid, and they both sighed
and shook their heads in unison.

"The reason," said the sheikh, lowering his voice, "is that of
late years there is no security for property.   If any Bedouin
happen to possess a fine horse, and it reach the Sultan's ears, the
animal is seized, and the owner receives no recompense.   So, to
escape this misfortune, he will rather cover his mare with the
coarsest pony, than seek a sire worthy of its ancient and high-
bred pedigree."

"Your case indeed is hard," said I.

"Hard!" said the Bedowee; "look at these scars on my ankles!
See where the iron entered into my flesh!   For seven long years
was I kept in prison: and why?   Ask him who put me there,
and even he will tell you that I treated with hospitality all who
visited Ibdowa, that I made large presents to kaid, basha, and
sultan.   In short, I was rich, and wealth* in this land of tyranny
is a crime: and many more, alas! have suffered for this, as well
as myself."

"Know, O Nazarene," he continued, "that our tribe are

* The most horrible tortures are resorted to for forcing confession of hidden wealth.   The victim is put into a slow oven, or kept standing for weeks
in a wooden dress; splinters are forced between the flesh and nail of the
fingers; two fierce cats are put alive into his wide trowsers, and the breasts
of his women are twisted by pincers.   Young children have sometimes been
squeezed to death under the arms of a powerful man, before the eyes of their
parents.

A wealthy merchant at Tangier, whose "*auri sacra fames*" had led him
to resist for a long time the cruel tortures that had been employed against
him, yielded at length to the following trial:—He was placed in the corner
of a room wherein a hungry lion was chained in such a manner as to be able
to reach him with his claws, unless he held himself in a most constrained
and unnatural position.

exempt from attending the sultan in his wars, or in his yearly progress through the country during the time of peace. This is granted us, because we have the privilege of escorting the annual caravan of pilgrims on their way to the holy Kaaba at Mecca. But now, alas! our services in this holy office are seldom required; and you English are the Bedouins of the present day, and in your ships and under your protection the Faithful are now conducted through the terrible sea to the regions of the East. You are the Bedouins, and well you deserve your wealth and power. I remember," continued the sheikh, "some hundred moons ago I was encamped with a party of friends on the coast of Reef; when we descried a boat leave a ship that was anchored at a little distance from the shore; and in it were seven Franks, who, having rowed to land, wandered along the beach. My companions seized their guns, and called upon me to follow them, determined on shooting the infidels. The sailors having observed this, made off to their boat and escaped, except one lad. He, not being able to reach the boat in time, was seized by my wild companions; who wished to kill him, or at least to keep him as a slave. On my coming up, I asked the lad of what nation he was. He understood my question, and replied, 'Ingliz;' and he looked at the same time so honest and so fearless, that I determined no one should harm the boy. So I spoke in his favour to those who had seized him; and when mild words failed, I swore by the beard of the Prophet, that rather than he should be injured, I would die in his defence. Having gained my point, I conducted him in safety to the water's side, where we made signals to his companions: they returned with the boat, and he embarked and was taken off in safety to the ship. I assure you, Christian, that I felt happier after having saved that boy's life, than at any other act I ever performed in my life."

"O virtuous sheikh!" said I, "God will repay you in the world to come."

Whilst thus conversing, the fatted lamb which the Arab chief had ordered to be killed, had been promptly metamorphosed into a stew, and was now placed before us in a large earthen dish by one of his attendants, whilst another bore a pile of flat loaves, greatly resembling Scotch bannock in form and taste.

During breakfast I spoke to the sheikh of the wonders of my

own country; and told him, to his astonishment, that we had many millions of Mahomedan subjects within our dominions, that our sultan was a young damsel, and that all the vast British empire was under her command.   The old sheikh laughed heartily at the idea of a maiden sovereign, and asked if she was pretty, and if she appeared before men.   I then gave a description of our Queen; and told him her Majesty had eyes like a gazelle and lips of coral, and that she could marry whom she pleased.

Upon this the Arab said, " Why does not the Sultan of Marocco, Mulai Abderrahman, ask her in marriage ?"

A party of mounted Bedouins galloping up interrupted our conversation, and relieved me from the necessity of answering this difficult question.

The horsemen proved to be a son of the sheikh and his attendants, on their way to a marriage some half-day's journey from the Dooar of Ibdowa.   They were all superbly dressed; their garments presenting a great contrast to their daily attire, which is in general of a mean appearance.

The sheikh, pointing to his son, who was a particularly handsome youth, said, " I have a good mind to send Abdallah to England.   He is of Shereefian descent.   Who knows but your Sultana might order him to wed her !"

Accompanied by the sheikh, I visited his brood mares; but they were all aged, and the colts under size.   The sheikh told me that he knew not of any horse, within five days' journey, of the fine description I required; but added that he would with pleasure travel even to Wadnoon in search of a fit animal, if I could obtain from the sultan a permission for his absenting himself from the tribe.

The weather having become cool, we took leave of our host, who endeavoured to persuade us to stay all night.   He loaded our animals with a present of three days' stock of fowls and other provision; and after a most friendly parting, we made the best of our way towards Oolad Sebaita.

About three in the afternoon we arrived at Had-al-Gharbeea, where we got into a hot current of wind from the north-east, which nearly suffocated us.   This extreme heat was occasioned, as we ascertained afterwards, by the firing of a large tract of brushwood many miles distant.   As we changed our course, we

L

suddenly emerged from the stifling current; and arriving at a well, slaked our parched throats, and those of our cattle, which had suffered even more than ourselves from the heat.

About five we pitched our tent amongst those of the sons of Sebaita. The sheikh, recognising me as a "son of the English," gave us a hearty reception; and having learnt the cause of my errand, troops of horses, mares and colts, were forthwith paraded before us; but all were of an inferior class of barb, and I was constrained to reject them.

This was a sad disappointment to me; for I well knew that, failing here, any further search would be useless; and therefore I was constrained, most unwillingly, to give up the object of my mission.

All that remained for me to do was to leave directions with the Sheikh of Sebaita to procure, if possible, a horse which should exactly answer to the description I gave him. He promised to exert himself to the utmost; but expressed his conviction, and so, indeed, did several other horse-dealers with whom I left similar instructions, that so perfect an animal as I required was not to be obtained.*

I wandered out in the evening with my gun, accompanied by the Hadj, and, in order to raise my spirits, which were somewhat of the lowest, blazed away among the partridges, which swarmed in the neighbourhood; whilst the Arabs, who witnessed the unheard of feat of killing a bird on the wing, actually screamed with delight at every successful shot.

Following a deep ravine, I arrived at an ancient well, which probably is of Portuguese construction; for within about half a mile of the spot I found the mutilated top of a large cross lying by the side of the way where two roads meet. A young woman was filling her pitcher at the well, and the Hadj stood aloof;

---

* In consequence of these instructions, a high-bred filly was after some delay procured, and sent to Tangier. It had many of the most valued qualifications of the breed; but it had never been broken in; and when subjected by me to the process, proved so violent a little creature, and put my neck so often into jeopardy, that it was deemed advisable to deprive her of the high honour which had been designed for her; and to renew the search for a more suitable animal. Subsequently, my father, when sent by her Majesty's government on a mission to the court of the sultan, at Fas, succeeded in obtaining a horse of the description required.

but I, being less scrupulous, approached, and thus addressed the maiden: " O heart-throbbing beauty ! may I not claim a draught from your pitcher, since my forefathers, the Room,* once adorned with buildings the limpid fountain, now the blessing of your Dooar?"

The girl, who had her back towards me, hearing a strange voice, suddenly looked round; when, seeing an armed and strange form, she abandoned her pitcher, and ran up the hillside like an antelope; but shortly stopped to take breath, and have a peep at the object of her dread. " Fear not, O maiden !" I cried; " I will run away myself, rather than you should be disturbed."

Having laid down my gun to calm her fears, I examined the well. The water was as clear as crystal. As I stooped down, a couple of large tortoises immediately came to the surface, and, approaching the brink, seemed to beg for bread, of which they are very fond. The Moors conceive that these animals purify the water; and it is not uncommon to find them in wells, where they become domesticated, and are fed by the hands of charitable passengers.

The Arab lass, seeing I was a harmless animal, soon took courage and returned. I asked her if she could give any history of the well: but all she knew was that it had been built by the Room.

During our flirtation she told me there would be a great feast in the village that evening; as a certain Mrs. Kador Abdelmalek had been delivered of a fine boy; and that as her mother and sisters were going to attend the feast, she should be left at home. As I returned to our tent, I met a large party of women who were going to this feast, shouting and screaming.

The Arab women are never so shy as the Moors of the towns; and much less so when in presence of a Nazarene than before a man of their own race. So the ladies halted to have a good stare at me; and I, on my part, was quite prepared to bear the brunt of their jests and raillery. There were amongst

---

* That is to say, *Romans;* but the term is more especially applied by the Moors to the early Christians: and as they have no knowledge of any more ancient race ever occupying their country, all old ruins, which are not of Mahomedan construction, are ascribed by them to the Room.

them many fine girls, with large black pearly eyes, long eye-
lashes, and slender figures with little feet and ankles. Such are
their charms. Some of them were dressed in caftans of red
cloth, embroidered in gold or silver, over which was a clear
muslin dress: the neck was covered with large strings of pearls
and rude bits of unwrought coral; and they were encumbered
with massive silver anklets and bracelets, little different in form
and weight from the manacles and fetters of our criminals.
Silk kerchiefs of Fas manufacture, of glaring colours, interwoven with golden thread, were placed one above the other in
pyramidical form upon their heads; and a rich sash of silk
encircled the waist above their hips. The poorer class were
decently attired in a simple white frock, reaching to the knees,
and girt with a small green band; the sleeves being large and
open. Their hair was in loose curls, hanging down the back,
but spangled with curious silver ornaments: all had their cheeks
highly rouged, or rather painted rose-colour; and their chins
tattooed in line and dot work. One dame I observed to have a
patch of red leather on her cheeks. Their dark eyes were rendered yet darker by alkohol,* and the tips of their fingers and
toes were dyed with henna. I put them in good humour by
declaring my unbounded admiration of them all: and the compliment was fully returned by one of the party, who was in the
way that ladies wish to be who love their lords, exclaiming,
" O God grant that my child be as fair as you, Christian!"
which, indeed, thought I to myself, is no extravagant prayer,
seeing that I was tanned a very respectable brown. But everything is comparative; and among these dark complexioned ladies
I have the great satisfaction of believing that I was esteemed a
very paragon of fairness.

* A preparation made up chiefly of the sulphuret of antimony.

CHAPTER XIII.

Monà—Gipsies—Mahomed Biteewy, the Sheikh of the Marksmen—The Death of the Lion—Wild Fowl—A Long Shot—Joas the Gunsmith—The Marksmen—Ain Dahlia—Story of the Reefian—Pirates—Death of the Bridegroom—The Feud—The Traitor—Return to Tangier—The Market.

AT our tent we found that a handsome *Monà* had been provided for us. The sheikh was grumbling at the expense he had been put to; though I learnt the rogue had levied a heavy tax on our account upon the whole Dooar, amounting to three times the value of the Monà, and pocketed the surplus. It was with good reason, therefore, that his neighbours had given him the nick-name of *Haffer*, or the Precipice: his relentless extortion being a gulf into which their goods were cast without a hope of benefit or recovery.

During our absence he had been complaining loudly to my companion, but finding that the Don did not understand him, the sheikh expressed to me his astonishment that a bearded man should not be able to speak Arabic. Pointing to his son, he said, " Shame upon thee, Nazarene; see, that child is only six years old, and understands every word I say."

Ere we retired to rest we were visited by some gipsy women; for it seems, even in this far country, that wandering race is found following the same pursuits and trade as their brethren in Europe. They told me my fortune, and spoke both of the past and the future; of the former very vaguely, though one of them certainly made some capital hits. The future prospect was drawn as bright as the glittering piece of money I put into her hand: but I fear my faith in the augury is too slight to entitle me to its fulfilment, this being, as I understood from the dark-eyed sibyl, an indispensable point.

On the following morning we made an early start; and, having threaded the pass of *Had-al-Gharbeea,* came in sight of

Dar-el-Clow, and the country around Sharf-el-Ahaab, our favourite sporting-ground. As the scene opened upon us, Sharky shouted a view-holloa, in which the Hadj joined most lustily; and goading on his mule till he reached my horse's side, he exclaimed, "*The well-fed** have rejoiced in our absence, but—may their great-grandfathers be burnt!—we will yet defile their graves. What say you, O Nazarene? let us pitch our tents hard by yonder lake, and send for old Irbeego and the rest of the pack."

"In truth," I replied, "I should be well pleased; but I cannot loiter on the road; for I have promised to be in Tangier this very night, if it please the Most High God."

"Remember you not," continued the Hadj, "that day of days we had near the hills of Shreewa, where we slew ten boars and six jackals? Ay, Sheikh Mohamed Biteewy headed the field well! and you and I were not among the slowest. By the truth of God, neither the cunning of Taleb Yooseff nor the sturdiness of the Father of Tusks availed that day; for the beaters kept good and steady line, and woe to the wild ones that showed themselves to the marksmen in the thicket, or to the swift-footed slokees† on the plain.

"How the Moslems stared as the camels, laden with the trophies of our sport, passed through the streets of our city 'protected of the Lord.' O, much sin was devoured by the Nazarenes at Tangier after that day's sport: and for that they ought to thank Sheikh Mohamed Biteewy. His eye never fails. Yes, he is a sheikh of sheikhs!"

"How long," I inquired, "is it since Biteewy was made a sheikh among the marksmen?"

"'T is half an age," he replied, "yea, ever since the former famine, that Biteewy was created sheikh; and well I know how first he acquired fame. If it please thee, Nazarene, with God's aid, I will relate the story, as often have I heard him tell it to his brother sportsmen."

I assented, and the Hadj thus commenced:—

* One of the innumerable Arab appellations given to the boar.
† The *Slokee* resembles in form the sleugh-hound of Scotland. The similarity in the name given to this species of dog in the two languages is somewhat curious.

" Sheikh Mohamed is a native of Tangier Baleea;* his father was a charcoal-burner, and God cut short his days when the beard of his son Mohamed first told that he had reached manhood.   On his death-bed he called unto him his son, and said, ' My son, I have nothing to give thee but my blessing and the gun of thy fathers.   It is thine now; and in a good cause it will never fail thee.   I recommend thee, my child, to God the everlasting, to Mohamed, the prophet of God, and to Seedy Boaza, who has ever been the patron saint of our family; and I command thee, above all other things, to visit forthwith his tomb in the forest of Manura.   Let neither man nor beast daunt thee; and Seedy Boaza will yet befriend a descendant of the Biteewys.'

" He had scarcely finished these words when his hour came, and Mohamed, closing his father's eyes, buried him ere the sun had set.

" Early the following day Mohamed rose; and taking down his father's gun, examined it, and found it to be in good condition: and then, like a dutiful son, he reflected on the words of his departed parent; and he swore, by the soul of his ancestors, that he would do as he had commanded him.   So he prepared forthwith for his journey, filling his wallet with bread and raisins, and girding his garments about his loins; and out he set for the shrine of Seedy Boaza, in the vast forest of Manura, some five days' journey south of Tangier.

" On taking leave of his friends, they warned him of the perils he would have to undergo in passing through districts infested with robbers and wild animals; especially lions, which abounded in the forest of Manura.

" Mohamed thanked them for their advice, but declared his determination to go on the pilgrimage to Seedy Boaza; and said he would trust to the saint's protection against all mishap.

" God favoured Mohamed on his journey; he reached the skirts of the forest of Manura on the evening of the fourth day: and as night was drawing on, the young pilgrim sought refuge and rest in a tree.

* Meaning ancient Tangier; a village opposite to the town of Tangier, and built near the site of the old Roman arsenal at the mouth of the river, of which there are still considerable remains. Tangier Baleea is believed by the Moors to be of much higher antiquity than the present town.

" Dreadful were the howlings of wild beasts, and the roar of lions shook the ground :—and that is a sound, O Christian ! to make faint the heart of man, be he never so stout.

" Morning dawned; and Mohamed, descending from his hiding-place, carefully examined the priming of his gun, which he had loaded with ball; and with his long dagger ready in his girdle, he continued his journey.

" He travelled on till the sun had reached mid-heaven, and told the hour of prayer; and he stopped and performed his prostrations near a brook, and when he had offered up a prayer for his safety, he again proceeded on his perilous journey. As he trudged on, he reflected on what had been told him about the lions and other wild beasts, of the truth of which during the last night he had had fearful proof; and as his mind dwelt upon such matters, he felt a creeping sensation come over him, and his hair stood erect, and the yellowness of his liver covered his skin.

" ' O Seedy Boaza,' he exclaimed, ' have I not put my trust in thee? and is not this foreboding a warning which thou hast sent me? It is: and I feel already that thy servant is in the presence of a foe.'

" He had hardly finished these words when he heard a rustling in the wood, as of some large animal; and presently, some thirty yards in front of him, a huge lion appeared in his path, fixing upon him his angry glance. Mohamed stopped short, and trembled from head to foot: but he soon took courage, and thus addressed the lion :—

" ' O dread sultan of the forest, I am a poor man, and on a pilgrimage to Seedy Boaza—May God have mercy on his soul ! Prythee, let me pass ! They tell me lions are generous and brave—I believe it; and I am indeed a harmless and inoffensive man.'

" On hearing this the lion shook his mane, as if he was satisfied; and turning round on the path, walked away from the man.

" ' Thank God !' said Mohamed: ' most true it is that the lion is a noble and sagacious animal.'

" But he had scarcely uttered these words, when again the lion halted, and, turning round, looked at Mohamed full in the face, and began to lash his tail. Then Mohamed thus again addressed the beast :—

" ' O yellow-haired shereef, think not that I have spoken aught against thee. I was only praising thee because thou hadst pity upon God's creature. I never thought or said that thou wast running away. I know thee to be brave: I know that thou fearest no living creature.'

" Upon this the lion left off lashing his tail, and turned away again : but still he kept upon the path along which Mohamed was journeying: and the young man, walking on with caution and as slowly as possible, ejaculated a prayer or two ; but speaking very low, for fear of making the lion angry.

" However, his prayers were soon put an end to : for all on a sudden the lion stopped for the third time, crouching with his head towards him, and his eyes glaring with fire, lashing his tail against his sides fiercer and fiercer.

" ' What!' said Mohamed, cocking his gun and holding it ready, ' must we then meet as foes? Know, O lion, that I have spoken to thee fair words ; but know also that I am a man ; and, being a man, above all the beasts of the earth.'

" The lion roared defiance, and sprung towards him. Mohamed took a steady aim and fired ; and the huge yellow monster rolled at his feet. The ball had entered the centre of the forehead, and gone through his brain.

" ' My father told me,' exclaimed Mohamed, ' that in a good cause this gun would never fail. Seedy Boaza has given me a sharp trial, but has not forgotten the family of Biteewy.'

" Mohamed now continued his journey; and at every rustle of the leaves he expected another encounter with some dread animal; but God befriended him; and he arrived without further harm in sight of the shrine of his patron saint: and, taking off his shoes, he approached the holy ground. As he drew near, he perceived a numerous party of huntsmen, whose long guns bristled in the neighbourhood of the sanctuary : and the oldest man of the party, stepping forward, thus addressed him :—

" ' O stranger, I see that thou comest from afar! Where are thy followers?'

" Mohamed pointed to his gun.

" ' What!' exclaimed the old hunter, ' dost thou mean that thou camest hither alone? Impossible! Lions infest the forest; dangers beset the sons of men. We are numerous; we have killed lions ere we reached Seedy Boaza's tomb. Speak then the truth, O stranger, that we may hear and understand.'

" ' I am from Tangier,' said Mohamed; ' I am alone. I have met a lion: I have slain him. I have come to worship at this shrine; and to-morrow I return to the house of my fathers.'

" ' If thou speakest the truth,' said one of the hunters, ' conduct us to the lion thou hast slain.'

" Mohamed made no reply; but led the way to the spot where the sultan of the forest lay dead. The hunters examined the lion's head for a good while; and then they embraced Mohamed, and called him Sheikh: and each hunter parted with some portion of his raiment and gave it to him; and some gave him money. And they loaded the young pilgrim with their favours; and they made him accompany them to their village, which was distant some two days' journey from the tomb of the saint.

" From that time Mohamed became a sheikh; and travelled throughout the country, teaching the young men to become marksmen. And so his fame spread far and wide, and his purse became full of gold. So he returned to the land of his forefathers, and took unto himself a wife; and ever since then Mohamed has lived happily, reflecting on the words of his father, and on the power of Seedy Boaza."

As we approached Dar-el-Clow, innumerable flocks of wild fowl were flying over head; and we saw a native sportsman make a most successful shot at a flight of ducks that had settled, killing three, which he brought to us for sale. The man had fired at a distance of not less than a hundred and thirty yards; and, although his shot were very large, the range was extraordinary.

On examining his gun I found the name Joaõ faintly engraved on the barrel, with a date, which was illegible. This Joaõ was a Portuguese, who had been taken prisoner by the Moors at the last battle with the Christians, not far from Alcassar Kebeer, in the year when their king Sebastian was

killed in the action; although some fond Portuguese suppose
that he is even to this day a wandering fugitive in the wilds of
Barbary!

Joaõ was conducted, with other of his fellow-prisoners, to the
royal residence of Meknas; and it is related that horrid cruel-
ties were practised upon the Christians. One of the methods of
torture employed was, to build them alive into the city walls,
which were under repair at the time. Whitened bones of these
and of former Christian prisoners are yet to be seen in the town
walls of Meknas, and they say in those of Sallee also. When
Joaõ's turn came, he begged for mercy; telling his persecutors
that he was a gunsmith; and, if they would spare him, he would
make a weapon which should be worthy the sultan of Marocco
himself. Information was forthwith given to the sultan of Joaõ's
handicraft; upon which the potentate ordered that the life of this
Nazarene should be spared, if he could fulfil his promise.

Joaõ now requested that a smith's shop and utensils should be
furnished him; and that no person should be allowed to overlook him while at work. The Nazarene artisan surpassed the
expectation of the sultan. The barrel was of twisted iron, a
mode of construction said to be unknown at that time in Marocco. As a reward for his services, Joaõ was appointed his
majesty's gunsmith; and his fame became great through this
country; and, as the Hadj, who was the gunsmith's biographer,
expressed himself, the hearts of all in the same trade " were
blackened with envy:" so they sought to ruin the Christian
favourite. But Joaõ continued to take the precaution of work-
ing alone; and thus prevented the mysteries of his art from
being discovered.

After a considerable lapse of time, however, the former gunsmith of his Shereefian Majesty petitioned to be restored to his
office; declaring that he could make as good a gun as the Nazarene. The Sultan promised to reinstate him if he could make
good his words; but to punish him severely, if he did not rival
the Nazarene.

Now Joaõ, it appears, was very particular about having his
shop frequently whitewashed; for the Sultan himself used to
visit the favourite artist while at work. His predecessor, having
endeavoured in vain to obtain admittance, and thus be enabled

to pry into the craft of the Portuguese, at length bribed the whitewasher, who was a Jew, to lend him his dress and brushes, and to let him know when next the Nazarene required his shop to be whitewashed.

The stratagem succeeded: for whilst Joaõ was busy at work, the Moor in disguise watched the process by which he formed the twisted barrel. Rejoicing at his success, the mallem * returned to his shop; and shortly afterwards presented a twisted gun-barrel to the Sultan, which was declared even superior to that of Joaõ: upon which his Shereefian Highness reinstated him in his former office, and the Christian was dismissed.

Joaõ mourned over his disgrace: but when he learned the deception which had been practised by the Moorish gunsmith, he was seized with despair, and, as the story goes, shot himself. His fame, however, is immortalized amongst all Moorish sportsmen, who prize the guns marked with his name above all others; and frequently their boar-hounds are called after the famous craftsman.

It was with barrels made by Joaõ that the famous marksmen Seedy Tayeb and Ben Geloon are said to have performed such incredible shooting feats.

It is related that, on one occasion, when these two marksmen, who had just returned from a hunting excursion, were seated together, discussing the shots that had been made during the day, Seedy Tayeb challenged Geloon to fire a shot with him. Geloon made no reply; but called to a young lad who was playing at foot-ball some fifty yards from them. The youth threw back the hood of his jelab, that he might approach him with due respect, for he was a Shereef: upon which, seizing his gun, he aimed at the lad and fired. The boy put his hand immediately to his head.

"Has any one hurt you?" cried Geloon. "Let us see your head."

The boy came up, and there was a slight graze where the ball had passed.

"What think you of that shot?" said Geloon to Seedy Tayeb. "Fire, if you can, one like it, at any of God's creatures, and yet do him no harm."

* Artisan.

Tayeb took his gun, and fired at the lad as he left them to return to his playfellows. This time the boy gave a slight scream, and put his hand to his ear.

"What's the matter?" cried Tayeb.

"Oh," said the boy, "somebody has torn my ear!"

The ball had shot away his large Moorish ear-ring.

We proceeded by the route we had formerly travelled until we came to Ain Dàhlia; where we were induced to take shelter in a neighbouring cave from the scorching rays of a midsummer sun. Here we were joined by a party of travellers going to Arzyla: and amongst them was one whose fine manly countenance and tall figure immediately attracted our notice. The Hadj told me he was a native of Reef, and an old acquaintance of his; but that of late years, in consequence of a feud, he had been obliged to leave his country. I beckoned to the man; and offering him some bread and fruit, of which we were making our meal, requested him to beguile the time by relating his adventures. He did so as follows:—

"O son of the English, I know your tribe are worthy of trust; and will therefore venture to speak of deeds of blood: but I pray thee to bridle thy tongue among the townsfolk; and let what thou shalt hear remain in thy secret heart. My father died when I was yet a child, leaving my mother with two sons, my brother and myself. He was about ten years older than I, and a finer fellow never breathed our mountain air. He was the raees of a large boat, carrying twenty oars, and capable of holding fifty armed men, if required to attack any trading vessels of the Nazarenes which might be becalmed off our coast or driven upon it. Often, as a lad, have I accompanied my brave brother —God have mercy on his soul!—in these expeditions; and dreadful was the conflict if the Nazarene happened to be armed. Our numbers, however, almost always prevailed: and, victory being gained, we put to death both crew and passengers, throwing their bodies overboard; but first taking the precaution to shave their heads, mutilate their faces, and strip their bodies, so that they might not be recognised.

"In our village there was a beautiful girl, a daughter of one of the wealthiest of our tribe. Her beauty was known to every man, for in Reef there is more confidence in the virtue of our women than with the people of towns; and therefore we allow them to go unveiled.

"My brother saw the maiden; and although the flame of love was alike kindled in the breast of the beautiful Ayèsha, his peace of mind was gone; for it was in vain he sought the girl in marriage from her father—she was promised to a wealthier man.

"Her marriage-day arrived, and the guests had assembled to feast and make merry. My brother was invited, but did not arrive until the end of the feast; and then, pale and haggard, he walked into the circle where the bridegroom was sitting, and thus addressed him:—'Know, O my rival, that God must this day judge between you and me. She whom you have chosen must be mine or no man's; say, wilt thou yield her to me, or dost thou prefer that our blood should run?' The bridegroom called on the guests to assist him: a struggle ensued; the bridegroom was stabbed to the heart, and near him soon lay my lifeless brother, shot by the pistol of one of the bridegroom's relatives.

"I was present at this horrid scene, but had not then completed my twelfth year; nor had I strength to resent the injury.

"In Reef, let it be known to you, O Christian! every man's gun is his law. We acknowledge no chief, no magistrate. The sultan himself is merely acknowledged in our country as the head of our religion.

"My mother, who doted upon her elder son, mourned for him to the day of her death: never did she cease, while we ate our meals together, to rebuke me for want of spirit in not seeking to revenge the blood of my brother: and, as I grew older, often did she taunt me in bitter words, lamenting that God should have given her such a worthless son as myself.

"All these sayings I kept secret in my heart; and long had I determined to revenge my brother's death. But I was yet too young to cope with the two surviving brothers of the murdered bridegroom: and well I knew that if I were unable to kill them both in one day, my own doom would be certain.

"At sixteen I married one whom I loved; and who, thank God, is yet alive, and has blessed me with many sons; who are ready to revenge the murder of their father, if such, after all, should be my fate.

" To my wife I confided my intentions of revenge. In vain did she beg of me to desist from the spilling of blood; and in vain also did the brothers of the murdered man, thinking I was yet too young to thirst after revenge, offer the price of blood to the large amount of two hundred *mitzàkal.* I spurned their offer, saying, ' God's will be done, both as to the past and the future.'

" One day I received information that one of the brothers intended to go to a neighbouring market, whilst the other would remain in the village. This separation was all that I wished for; and I at once determined upon the execution of what I had so long designed.

" On meeting at our mid-day meal my mother and wife, I said to my mother, ' Prepare all we possess of value, and make ready for a flight to the sanctuary of Mulai Abd-Selam. After to-morrow Reef can no longer be our home.'

" My mother understood my words, and, falling on my neck, called me for the first time her dear son; and then taking down my brother's gun, which had hung unused and dusty for many a day on the walls of our house, she blessed it, and offered up a prayer for my success. My wife, poor creature, on the contrary, never ceased to weep, fearing for me, and her own boys too, the fatal consequences of renewing the feud.

" The following morning, accompanied by my wife, I went to a spot where the villagers were accustomed to assemble; taking with me my gun, which, as thou knowest, Christian, is seldom out of a Reefian's hand. Here I learned that one of the brothers had already gone to a market some three hours distant from our village; and not far from me I saw the other brother seated near an open metamor,* the contents of which he was inspecting. Two other persons only were present, most of the villagers having gone to the market.

" I observed the object of my revenge look round every now and then, as if watching my movements; for both he and his brother, I knew, had become suspicious of me. Taking advan-

---

* The underground granaries yet in universal use by the Moors of West Barbary, being the same in form and name as those introduced into Western Europe by the old conquering Saracens; and which have so strangely puzzled both antiquaries and etymologists.

tage of a moment when his back was turned towards me, I took
off my jelab and put it over my wife, whose teeth were chattering
with fright; and desired her to sit still as she valued my life.
Then, taking my gun, I approached him, dodging so as to avoid
detection: he looked round more than once towards the place
where I had been sitting, but perceiving a figure seated in my
dress, he thought I had not moved. Having got within fifteen
paces of my object, I presented my gun and shot him through
the back. Several people came out on hearing the report; but,
having perceived the cause, not a word was said. They knew I
had done my duty as a Reefian.

" Returning to my wife, I resumed my dress, and desired her
to hasten to our hut and tell my mother what I had done; then
to saddle the mule and ass, and, taking the best of our effects, to
set out on the journey to Mulai Abd-Selam. I told her to assure
my mother that I would join them before night. Reloading my
gun, I now hastened in the direction of the market; and met my
victim's brother returning with other Reefians: they inquired
whither I was going so fast. I told them that we were in want
of salt at the house, and I was hastening to market that I might
buy some and return before night. One of the party, telling me
I should be late, offered to share his. I desired only an excuse
for joining them, and accepted his offer. Then, watching my
opportunity, I fell back a little behind the rest, and shot the
remaining brother through the back. His companions, none of
whom were related to him by blood, merely fired their guns off,
not aiming at me; for too prudent is a Reefian to commence a
feud without a sufficient cause.

" At night I joined my wife and mother, and, having remained
some days at Mulai Abd-Selam's tomb, we came to the neighbourhood of Tangier, near which place we have dwelt ever since;
and are now subject to the laws of our Prophet and the Prince of
Believers.

" Only on one occasion has my life been attempted by a cousin
of my former enemies; who, too dastardly to come himself, hired
for a large sum a Reefian who had formerly been my friend. This
man undertook to seek me in my own house, eat my bread, and
murder me when the occasion offered. The very day the murderous hireling arrived I was warned by my wife, who told me

she liked not his looks.　I did not listen to her counsel, but continued to treat my former friend with hospitality : until one day my wife brought me a bit of paper she had found in his wallet. On it was written the contract for my blood, at the price of one hundred and fifty mitzàkal.　Struck with indignation at the treachery, I went immediately to the villain; showed him the proof of his guilt; and seizing his gun and dagger, I broke them both into pieces; telling him that his having eaten with me the bread of peace was his sole security against my delivering him up to the hands of justice.

"Since that time I have lived in peace; and now, thank God, have many a stout heart under my roof to revenge, if need be, their father's quarrel."

The Reefian having finished his tale, we remounted, and arrived at Tangier about the *Asa*, or hour of evening prayer.

It was market-day, and the large Sok was crowded with villagers from the neighbouring hills, and Arabs with their camels from the plains, forming a gay and busy scene.　As we passed to our dwellings we were hailed with the kindly salutations of many of our Moorish friends, gaily crying out to us, "*Hamdoolillah Salamah*" (we thank God for your safe return).

M

CHAPTER XIV.—(APPENDIX.)

John Davidson—His Qualifications and Personal Appearance—Superstitious
Feelings—Imprudence—Moorish Suspicions—Reception by the Sultan—
Reaches Wadnoon—Murdered at Swekeya—Mr. Willshire's Letter—The
Sheikh's Letter—Suggestions.

JOHN DAVIDSON deserves to be placed high in the long list of
those energetic travellers who have sacrificed their lives in the
cause of science. In the year 1835, he formed the bold design
of penetrating to Timbuctoo by the direct route from Wadnoon
—a line of approach never before attempted by any European,
and one which it was well known was beset with imminent
danger.

Few persons could have been better fitted than Davidson for
this arduous undertaking. He was a man of high moral and
personal courage, combined with great calmness of temper and
affability of manner. He possessed a general knowledge upon
most subjects, and very considerable skill in chemistry and medicine; acquirements which are of the greatest importance to the
traveller in those countries, and which, even if he does not
possess them, he is frequently obliged to profess; for the Nazarene is always looked upon as a skilful doctor, and to refuse the
assistance of his art would be attributed by the Africans to worse
motives than mere ignorance.

Davidson was a fine-looking man, with an extremely intelligent countenance, and an expression that would tell even the
savage of Africa that he was an honourable and brave man: the
fairness of his skin and the redness of his hair were, however,
somewhat against him in the estimation of the sunburnt inhabitants of Africa: for though among the people of the city of
Fas, and those of the northern districts of West Barbary, the
"*Zaar*" (the fair), as they are called, are frequently to be
found, being probably the descendants of the large body of
Goths who crossed the Straits, still the word *Zaar* is used as an

opprobrious term; the prejudice being that a fair man is not to be depended upon.

Davidson was a tolerable linguist; but his knowledge of Arabic, especially of the Mogrebbin dialect, was very limited; and on this acconnt he was obliged to engage a Hebrew of Tetuan to accompany him as interpreter to the court at Marocco.

While residing at Wadnoon he suffered dreadfully from a disease brought on by the hot poisonous wind called *simoom*, which first attacked his eyes with ophthalmia, and then his throat; the palate falling, as he expressed himself. Finding no relief from his own remedies, he was obliged to resort to those of the country, which consisted in a stick covered with tar being poked down his throat, and his inhaling the fumes of boiled tar; and such were his sufferings, that in one of his letters he writes, " I would readily step into the grave."

In the work entitled ' John Davidson's African Journal,' printed by his brother for private circulation, I find in a note the following vivid description of the simoom, written by the traveller at the time :—

" To describe this awful scourge of the desert defies all the powers of language. The pencil, assisted by the pen, might perhaps afford a faint idea of it. Winged with the whirlwind and charioted in thunder, it urged its fiery course, blasting all nature with its death-fraught breath. It was accompanied by a line of vivid light that looked like a train of fire, whose murky smoke filled the whole wide expanse, and made its horrors only the more vivid. The eye of man, and the voice of beast, were both raised to heaven, and both then fell upon the earth. Against this sand-tempest all the fortitude of man fails, and all his efforts are vain. To Providence alone must he look. It passed us, burying one of my camels. As soon as we rose from the earth, with uplifted hands to heaven for its preservation, we awoke to fresh horrors. Its parching tongue had lapped the water from our water-skins, and having escaped the fiery hour, we had to fear the still more awful death from thirst."

Davidson was not skilled in the use of fire-arms; which accomplishment, indeed, often gains a stranger the friendship of barbarians, either through fear of your prowess or respect for you as a warrior. He was of a very fanciful disposition, and often indulged in superstitious feelings; which, though he affected to laugh at them, had, I suspect, much influence on his mind.

I accompanied this ill-fated traveller as far as the town of Rabat, a port of Marocco, about 120 miles south of Tangier ; and was most anxious to have proceeded with him throughout his entire journey ; but, fortunately for me, my family insisted upon my giving up the design. Had I continued with him, my fate must have been the same as his.

On taking leave of him at Rabat, I gave him a pistol-holster, which I used to wear slung, after the Turkish fashion, at my side, and which Davidson had taken a fancy to. This holster had belonged to a native of Tunis, who was supposed to have taken an active part in the murder of Laing, the African tra-veller. On Davidson's arrival at Mogador, he wrote to me to say that Laing's ghost had appeared to him, and rebuked him for wearing the holster of the pistol that belonged to his murderer ; and that, owing to this warning, he was about to send me my gift back. Davidson, at times, dwelt much upon what had been told him by some fortune-telling woman in Russia, respecting his life and death, foretelling, as he said, many things that had since come to pass ; and he particularly alluded to her prophecy of his death in Africa, at a period, as I understood him, when he had no intention of penetrating into the interior.

Davidson started from the very first in a manner which tended to throw impediments in his way. He had published to the world his intended journey ; and the fame of his coming was bruited about at Gibraltar long before he appeared: and that famous Rock has always been a hotbed for engendering mis-chievous reports ; which, if connected in any way with Marocco, are sure to find their way over the Straits, and thence to the court at Marocco, in an exaggerated and distorted form. He had been received at Gibraltar with great kindness by the autho-rities and inhabitants, and fêted during the time he was there ; a compliment which the enterprising traveller well deserved ; but such hospitality was ill-timed and unfortunate, for the greater the importance given at Gibraltar to his character and proceed-ings, the more impediments was he certain to meet with on the other side of the Straits: and thus it proved ; for from that time he was looked upon by the Moors as an agent sent by the British government to inquire into the state of the country, its productions and capabilities; and it is more than probable they suspected that his mission was connected with plans of future conquests.

Davidson brought with him a letter of recommendation from his Majesty William IV. to the Sultan of Marocco,* stating that the object of his travels was purely scientific. The delivery of this letter to the Sultan was in itself an unwise measure; for it stamped the bearer as an agent of the British government, and consequently Davidson was looked upon with a jealous and suspicious eye by the Moorish court. The Sultan of Marocco little knows or cares about scientific pursuits. It would never enter into the mind of a Moor, not even the most enlightened, that any man would expose his life by travelling through the wild tracts of West Barbary, or attempt to penetrate into the land of deserts and death, solely for the love of travel and science. Gain, the Moor would argue, must be his object; and for this alone, would he conclude, the Englishman was travelling in countries where he exposed his life.

To a like course of reasoning among the wealthy merchants of Fas and Tâfilelt may the death of the unfortunate traveller be attributed. These traders, and others of the principal towns of Marocco, have long held in their hands the monopoly of the trade of Northern Africa, consisting in gold-dust, ivory, ostrich-feathers, &c. With what eyes must they, then, have viewed the man whom they considered the emissary of a great commercial nation, with whom these goods have long been an object of traffic! The natural inference of these Moors would be—This man is going into the interior to enter into an arrangement with agents there for sending the productions of the country to some more direct port of export than those of Marocco; and if he succeed in this object, he will destroy our trade.

* Davidson was sent from Gibraltar to Tangier in his Majesty's brig-of-war Jaseur; and was landed under a salute of eleven guns, as bearer of a royal letter. Those who conferred this mark of honour on the worthy traveller thought that they were rendering him a service by raising his importance in the eyes of the Moors; but I remember feeling, as I heard the roar of the cannon echoed back by the hills—over which he was so soon to pass, never to return—that these were the death-guns of the gallant traveller.

Impressed with views such as these, and callous in the com-
mission of crime, it is easy to suppose that these traders would
have endeavoured to prevent, either by fair means or foul, the
return of such a traveller to his own country, as his success
might ensure their ruin.

If the Sultan and his court, who seemed to have taken an
interest in Davidson during his stay at the city of Marocco in
consequence of his engaging manners and valuable acquirements,
felt disposed to humour the Nazarene, and to promote a scheme
which they must have looked upon, even when viewing it more
favourably, as the wild fancy of a mad infidel, other enemies
were at work; and these, no doubt, were the Maroquine merchants, who necessarily viewed with a jealous eye every step
Davidson took towards the interior.

The Sultan warned the traveller not to attempt to penetrate
farther than those regions where his control extended; and
Davidson even received an order not to go beyond Tarudant, as
he himself stated to his brother, in his letter of the 7th March,
1836: and though a kind of promise was held out to him that
facilities would be subsequently rendered him for putting his
journey to Timbuctoo into execution, I very much doubt the
sincerity of such a promise; or that even with the Sultan's
authority and assistance he would ever have proceeded farther
than Wadnoon. A flat refusal is not the Moor's policy; but
procrastination and awaiting the effect of events is their safe and
wily system.

When Davidson prosecuted his journey under the countenance
of the sheikh, and not that of the Sultan, all responsibility was
removed from the Sultan's shoulders, even could it have been
proved that that potentate had received some intimation of the
murderous scheme of the Tâfilelt traders: for, should the British
government have in any way taken up the circumstances connected with Davidson's death, the Sultan could have clearly
shown that he had protested against the wild scheme in which
the Englishman had embarked.

Greatly is it to be lamented that he did not list n to the
counsels of those who foresaw the danger of the plan he had
formed for penetrating into the interior, rather than to the
advice and sanguine expectations held out by many of his

friends; who thought that the difficulties which were pointed out to him were put forward with other motives than those of a hearty desire for the success of the spirited traveller. In several letters which I received from him, when he was residing at the court of Marocco and at the port of Wadnoon, he frankly admitted the soundness of the advice which had been given to him on this subject by my father and several other persons well enabled to form a correct opinion. Most painful indeed was the tenour of some of these letters; for though Davidson possessed a wonderful elasticity of spirits and undaunted determination, still, foreseeing when too late the full extent of the dangers that must attend him, he predicted his own certain doom: but at the same time he said, "I will not turn back, to be pointed at by the world as the man who had undertaken to accomplish what he dared not even attempt."

Davidson arrived at Tangier on the 13th of November, 1835; where he remained for some weeks awaiting the answer of the Sultan for permission to proceed on his journey.

The Sultan having at length replied to his application by desiring him to come to the city of Marocco, and having provided him with an escort of ten horsemen, as a compliment to the bearer of a king's letter, he started on the 26th of December, accompanied by Mr. J. Crusenstolpe,* the Swedish vice-consul, and myself. The first town we visited was Laraiche, which we left on the 29th, and reached Mehedeea, a small sea-port town, on the 1st of January, 1836, and on the 2nd arrived at Rabat, where, on the 5th, Mr. Crusenstolpe and myself took leave of the traveller, and returned to Tangier.

Davidson's next point was Dar-al-baida. The intermediate country was then in a disturbed state; and a regular escort of four hundred cavalry was appointed to attend all travellers to and fro on stated days of the week. Davidson mistook the nature of this numerous escort; and imagined that it had been sent by the Sultan as a compliment to himself.

From Dar-al-baida he journeyed to Azamor; and arrived at Marocco on the 13th of January. The Sultan gave him an

---

* This gentleman, who is a profound Arabic scholar, has lately published an excellent translation of the Koran into Swedish, accompanied by valuable notes explanatory of the laws and customs of the Mohamedans.

audience; and on more than one occasion, I believe, received him in private. He made him a present of a horse, and all such other gifts as are usually bestowed on persons visiting that court; and also a regular supply of provisions for himself and attendants.

Davidson acquired great fame in the capital as a medical man, and attended the first people of the court, as well as the ladies of the sultan's harem, and other ladies of note ı and in addition to this, performed numerous acts of charity in the line of his profession.

The sultan endeavoured to persuade him to remain at Marocco as his medical adviser; and no doubt he would have been well treated in that capacity: but the traveller would not accede to this proposal: he obtained his leave of audience on the 17th of February, and proceeded on his journey. He crossed part of the Atlas Mountains; visited a singular and warlike tribe of Jews there, who are almost independent of the sultan; and arrived at Mogador on the 25th of February; from which port he departed on the 23rd of March, and arrived at Wadnoon, viâ Agadeer, on the 22nd of April. After a long and most vexatious detention at Wadnoon, suffering from climate and other causes, he entered into a pecuniary arrangement with the sheikh for prosecuting his journey to Timbuctoo; and at length, about the middle of November, set forward on his ill-fated journey.

Davidson is supposed to have been murdered at Swekeya* by a party of fifteen persons, of the tribe of El Harib, whilst awaiting the caravan, having at this time with him only twelve of the Tajacauth tribe. The Sheikh Beyruche, in a letter which he addressed to Mr. Willshire, Her Majesty's Vice-Consul at Mogador, announcing the death of the Tibeeb (Doctor), as Davidson was called, says:—

"El Harib did not go that route but to kill him; and we have heard that the merchants of Tâfilelt had given money to El Harib to murder him. Tâfilelt is only distant one or two days' journey from the usual place of abode of the tribe of El Harib."

The sheikh, in a subsequent letter, retracted this assertion

---

* Swekeya is, I believe, near the southern confines of Eguedec, sixteen days' journey from Tatta, and ten from Toadaguy.

about the guilt of the Tâfilelt merchants ; and this was a very natural course for him to take ; for the deed of blood was done, and could not be remedied ; and though he imprudently, at the first, proclaimed the guilt of El Harib, and at one time even threatened to be revenged on that tribe for their perfidy ; on reflection he must have been aware that, should his accusation and threats reach the ears of the Tâfilelt people, it would create him many and powerful enemies. The Arab's policy is always to employ soft words, however much they may be contradicted by his actions.

The following extracts from letters written on the subject by Mr. Willshire give, there is every reason to suppose, the most correct details of the murder of the poor traveller :—

" Mr. Davidson and party were first met by some of the tribes of Howbet and Ait Atta, who took from him some money, and allowed the party to proceed. The party reached Swekeya ; where they rested, to wait for the caravan to come up. On the third day, a party of fifteen or more of the tribe of El Harib arrived at the resting-place ; and, after the usual salutations, inquired of Mohamed El Abd to show him the watering-place ; who, leaving his musket behind, and the rest of the Harib sitting down, accompanied him over the sand-hills ; and when out of sight, hearing a report of a musket, Mohamed El Abd asked what had been done ; when the Harib replied, his party had shot the Christian. He complained bitterly, and said he would rather they had murdered him. It is stated, that when Mohamed El Abd went away, one of the Harib pretended to examine his gun ; and seized the opportunity to take aim, and shot Mr. Davidson, who was sitting on the ground a short distance from the party ; who immediately began to plunder and seize everything belonging to Mr. Davidson, allowing Mohamed El Abd to keep possession of what property belonged to him, obliging him first to make oath on the Koran that the caravan was not met by the Harib, but had gone on to Timbuctoo, with which Abú, the companion of Mr. Davidson, travelled."

In another account it is stated that when the Harib shot Davidson, they proceeded to plunder his baggage, tearing and destroying all his *books and papers.*

From these statements it evidently appears that the Harib had other views than mere plunder; for those who made the first attack were satisfied with robbing the travellers; but the Harib, unprovoked by any resistance, murdered the unfortunate Christian, and then destroyed *all his books and papers;* whilst they allowed " *Mohamed El Abd to keep possession of what property belonged to him;*" and I have little doubt that those who hired these ruffians had given them especial instructions not only to make away with the traveller, but to destroy all his papers; which they would fear might contain information likely to be injurious to their trade, should they reach the Nazarenes. This opinion is confirmed by the fact that most of his other property has been recovered : and very lately I had the melancholy satisfaction of receiving, through the kindness of the brother of the lamented traveller, a small silver pedometer which I had lent him. There is no reason to believe that there was any treachery on the part of the Sheikh Beyruche, or of the Arabs attending Davidson, notwithstanding the apparent want of spirit of the Tajacauth who accompanied him, in revenging upon the Harib, on the spot, the death of their Nazarene companion. It was against their interest to have been a party to the murder, putting aside the friendship that had subsisted between the Sheikh and Davidson. The plain language in which the former justifies his conduct, in a letter addressed by him to a certain Sidi Hadj Abibe, is sufficient, I think, to exculpate him from having been privy to the murder or robbery.

The following is an extract from this letter :—

" The words you report, that we had arranged with the Harib to betray him (Davidson)—such doings are not our ways; nor could we degrade ourselves to do so ; every one, God will reckon with for the words he utters.

" For four days we neither ate nor drank, and have sworn by all that is sacred to be revenged. Whenever the Harib are to be found, in the tents or on the road, our tribe shall plunder and kill them.

" As regards the property of the Tibeeb, if any articles remain in the hands of the Tajacauths, they will reach you. God knows how much we have grieved about him; but, God be praised, we did not leave anything undone for the safety of the Tibeeb. We did not think the Harib would turn traitors to any person sent by us. This has been done by the traders of Tåfilelt, who had bribed the Harib to kill him. God's will be done: the facts will be known when the two horsemen return, whom we have despatched to Tajacauth, and which will be sent to you.— Peace."

The advice given to Davidson, by those who were sincerely desirous that he should undertake his perilous journey in the manner least likely to endanger his life, was, that he should have totally abandoned his first plan; that he should have even returned to England, and encouraged a rumour that he had altogether given up the idea of his African travels, confiding alone to the most trustworthy persons his future mode of proceeding; which, should he persist in the scheme of penetrating to Timbuctoo through West Barbary, was sketched out for him as follows : —

" To have remained in England until he was no longer talked of as the African traveller, and during that time to have improved his knowledge of the Arabic: on leaving England, to have changed his name, which was already too well known; to have avoided Gibraltar and Tangier, where many persons would have recognised him, and to have embarked on board a sailing vessel for Mogador, of which there are several that leave London every year, and to have landed at that port, in the capacity of a petty trader possessing some little knowledge of medicine, but at the same time to have been careful not to have rendered himself conspicuous by the practice of his art so as to have dazzled the natives, or to have caused his name to have been talked of by the Frank merchants or agents for Foreign Powers; among whom, as in every small town, there would always be found busy-bodies, who can do no good, but much harm. We also recommended that he should have settled at Mogador for some time, studying the Mogrebbin dialect, and picking up, if possible, the language of the African tribes through which he would have to pass, and acquiring at the same time information respecting the interior, and a knowledge of the habits and character of the people; and whilst carrying on a petty trade, he should have endeavoured to have formed acquaintances, and make friends with the Arabs who accompany the kafflas."

To Mr. Willshire, the British Vice-Consul at Mogador, he might have confided his plans, and I know no man in Marocco more capable of giving sound advice to the traveller in those regions, or more zealous in rendering every service in his power for the benefit of geographical knowledge. Mr. Willshire is held in high repute by the natives, among whom, no doubt, he has many good friends : in fact I believe Davidson was indebted to him, on more than one occasion, for introductions to those who afterwards proved his more worthy acquaintances.

After having obtained a sufficient knowledge of the interior, and having established commercial connections with the traders, he might have joined a kaffla for the ostensible purpose of purchasing goods on his own account ; assuming for safety, and to avoid notoriety, the dress of the country, and taking with him only such necessaries of life as would not have excited the avarice or curiosity of the Arabs : and, above all, he should have travelled with some native of good character, who was respected by his brethren, and with whom he should have previously formed a tie of friendship, or to whom he had rendered some important medical service : for, faithless and treacherous as are the tribes of North Africa, like most half-civilized people, and much as they hold the Nazarene in detestation, yet I could bring forward instances, which have occurred to myself, where these men have proved that they were worthy of a Christian's friendship and confidence ; and that too at moments when life and death were at stake, and when they were opposed to those of their own faith, and to superior numbers. But had I not in these cases formed a previous tie of friendship, and had I not broken the bread and drank the milk of peace with them, my protectors would have been the first, under similar circumstances, to have turned their arms against the adversary of their faith.

Had Davidson prudently adopted measures such as these, he could have penetrated into the interior to Timbuctoo, or even farther if he had pleased : nobody would have heard of his journey ; or if they had, they would not have thought it worth while to murder a mere petty trader of Mogador, who did not interfere in any way with them ; and who had every appearance of being a needy man, and of having, on that account, undertaken the journey himself, instead of sending an agent. His character of a Christian would have been the principal obstacle in his way: for although, if he had assumed the character of a Jew, he might have been abused, he would have been certain of escaping with his life; for the Jew is the Rayah, or tributary subject, of Marocco, where, unlike the countries in the East, there are no Christian subjects. In Marocco the religion of the Nazarene is supposed to be that of idolatry; and those Moslems who, living in districts about Tangier, can, when they please, peep into the Papist chapel, adorned with images and pictures, are confirmed in this opinion.

Not only are the Nazarenes confounded with those against whom their prophet launched such severe anathemas, but the traditions of the Crusaders, and of the expulsion from Spain of their ancestors,* keep up these feelings of enmity against the Christians; who are supposed to be always plotting the destruction of the Mohamedans: and, therefore, to kill a Christian is considered a meritorious act, and one which ensures Paradise to them: and it must be owned that, in following out this barbarous theory, they are merely retaliating upon us the misdeeds of our forefathers.

The most fortunate thing that could have occurred to Davidson would have been to have made acquaintance, whilst residing at Mogador, with some of the chiefs of the interior. Many years ago, when I was too young to have undertaken the journey with any prospect of useful result to geographical science, I made friends with some of the chiefs, or princes, of the Soudan country, one of whom was the brother of the reigning prince of Shingitti: they were returning from a pilgrimage to Mecca, and had experienced during their transit hither much kindness and assistance from British officers. These chiefs were most anxious that I should have accompanied them to their own country; and offered to take me on to Timbuctoo, if I had any desire to go there. Finding that I did not fancy the journey as one of pleasure, they endeavoured to tempt me by saying that as many baggage-animals as I chose to take should return with me laden

---

* There are descendants of the Moorish families of Granada now residing in Tetuan and Fas, who still preserve the keys, and it is said also the title-deeds, of the houses of their Mauro-Spanish ancestors, in the hope that the Arabs will yet return as conquerors to Spain.

with gold-dust, or any other productions of the interior I might choose. On my adverting to the dangers which would attend the journey, one of the party said, " Four hundred of my blood and tribe bear my name: they shall all perish ere the least insult be offered to you, even were you to travel with a jewelled crown upon your head." I found these chiefs far less fanatical than the people of Marocco: they were skilled in Arabic literature, and spoke a dialect resembling that of the Arabs of Mecca.

Supposing Davidson to have assumed the character of a trader, it would have been necessary for him to have used great caution in making notes of his travels whilst under the active eyes of his companions: indeed it would have been better for him to have trusted to his memory until he arrived at Timbuctoo: unless he had resorted to stratagem, and availed himself of his medical functions; which, superstitious as the Moors are, he might easily have done.

Some one or other of the persons composing the kaffla would most probably have been ill, or might easily have been induced to consider himself so; and Davidson could have asserted the necessity of consulting the stars on his case, and of recording their decrees: and whilst professing to do so, he could have made whatever notes and astronomical observations he pleased, without molestation, or exciting suspicion. A barbarian is always fond of being doctored; and a few bread pills, with some incomprehensible words muttered over them, would have been all he need have administered to the imaginary invalid. Whilst attending the ailments of the members of the kaffla, Davidson might have acquired the good will and friendship of them all: and once at Timbuctoo, his return would have been a far easier matter: but he would still have found it his interest to have played the part of a trader, purchasing a sufficient quantity of goods to blind the natives as to his real objects.

Davidson committed, I conceive, a great error in bringing with him from London Abú Bekr as his companion. Putting out of the question the physical incapability and want of moral courage of that very excellent and enlightened negro, the circumstance of his being connected with the reigning families in Soudan not only rendered his return to that country dangerous to himself, but compromised the life of his protector; who, I think, took a very mistaken view on the subject in his letter to the Duke of Sussex, dated 3rd of July, 1836, in which he said, " My companion" (Abú Bekr) " begs most respectfully to present his duty; and hopes your royal highness will deign to receive the few lines from his pen which he begs me to inclose. I am sorry to say I have great fears for his health : he cannot bear fatigue, and has been attacked with ophthalmia. *The whole of the Soudan people know him, and tell me he will prove a certain passport, that he is a cousin of Hamed Libboo, and another of his cousins, Ali, called Koutoribu, the Warrior, is now king of Kong, and that many of his relations are at Kong, all rich and in power.*"

When in Marocco, although his master gained the good wishes of many for having liberated and cherished a Mohamedan, Abú lost caste, as having been in Christian thraldom, and, by continuing to live with Davidson, became an object of constant suspicion to all Moslems: and should he have attempted to return to Europe after visiting the interior, he would have endangered both his own life and that of his protector; for the Sultan of Marocco looks upon himself as the rightful sovereign of all persons professing Mohamedanism.

The health of Abú was also a constant source of trouble to his patron: he was a timid creature, and constantly embarrassing Davidson by his want of energy and moral courage. Even before we arrived at Rabat he appeared to be suffering from the effects of the journey; and often declared to me in confidence that he wished himself again in England, and that he never would have undertaken the journey had he not considered it to be a debt of gratitude to Davidson; that he had no desire to visit his native country, and that his sole hope was to return ere long to Europe, and live quietly amongst an enlightened and civilized people.

Abú Bekr was a good Arabic scholar, but understood very little of the vulgar tongue. He had a great contempt for the Moors; and was especially disgusted by their ignorance and faithlessness.

Little or nothing has been heard of him since Davidson's

murder, and there appears every reason to suppose that he is dead.

I attribute the failure of all our travellers in their attempts to penetrate into the interior of Africa to the notoriety with which their perilous journey has been undertaken; thus exciting the jealousy of both *natives* and *foreigners*. I have not much faith in Caillie's account. He may have been at Timbuctoo : but if he was, accuracy as a draftsman does not appear to have been his forte. I showed to a native of Timbuctoo the sketch he gives of that town ; and the man neither recognised the forms of the houses nor the situation of the town itself; although, on being shown other drawings of cities and villages with which he was also acquainted, he at once named the places which they represented.

Referred to at page 50.

Ya Du Du ya foom el Hatsem ya Lel - lat - si -

Ya Lel - lat-si, ent-si be - ia ua - na - ha hem

Ya Lel - lat - si, Ya Lel - lat - si, Ktseer h - beeb

ui gra - mi, Ya Lel - lat - si, Ya Lel - lat - si.

TRANSLATION.

O Dedu! Your mouth is like a ring. O my lady! O my lady!
You are courted by all, but I am your lord. O my lady! O my lady!
Much love for you, my sweetheart.

N

CPSIA information can be obtained at www.ICGtesting.com
Printed in the USA
LVOW09s1546210116

471718LV00010B/335/P